# THE CRIES

*also by*
*Joseph Adams*


Yeats and the Masks of Syntax

THE CRIES

a novel

JOSEPH ADAMS

for Judy and Paul

# TABLE

**What was it all for, Romano?** Don't you ever ask yourself? If you don't, you should. We all should. I mean, did we do any good? I have no answers. Just bad ones. Maybe it was for nothing. Maybe it was all just a bloody waste of time. That's possible. But back then most of us never really thought like that. It wasn't for nothing. There was a story we told ourselves. It was a lie or a fable. But we needed that fable. We were dead lost without it. You try to fool yourself to get through. You wear these blinders against the horror. And then you look for the light. You look down the tunnel and you look for the light. Anything to get you through. Even you have to admit it wasn't easy. We tried in our different ways, didn't we? Totally different ways, you and me. That's an old story and a very sad one. But, tell me, what do you honestly think it amounted to? What was the point? Did it have to be so painful to bear? If you come right down to it, do you think either of us really knew what we were doing or why we were doing it? I know I failed a lot of them. I don't think I need to apologize. I failed most of them, to be honest. I know that better than you do. The pain of all that. But they're a part of me now and they won't ever leave me. Does that surprise you? And do you know what else I came to realize? They were the essence of the human to me. I know that now and I think about it. I think about it all the time.

◆

I'm sure you couldn't care less about any of this. I doubt if you could even imagine what it felt like, or what it would mean to me when I'd taken everything in. That's too much to ask. I never grasped it myself when it was all going on. Every day I used to show up at the brownstone my feelings going right through me. Nights I'd come out onto the street intoxicated. The air would hit me and the feelings. It's hard to imagine. I was almost stupefied by what we were doing, or thought we were doing. Even the place was a part of it, our leafy block, the ratty old building. It was tremendous. I'm still trying to sort it all out. But you don't think about any of it now, would be my guess. Why would you? There's no need to. But there I was. There I was, right in the midst of it. And you know something? Sad and painful as it was, it was actually beautiful in a lot of ways. I thought it was beautiful for quite a while, that first year anyway. As much as things would get so truly horrendous later.

◆

And, yes, I remember them. My patients. My so-called patients. The lot of them. What a world. Their faces, their voices, what they told me, how they lived, what they felt, everything. Their grief, their tears, their lies, dreams, rage, terror, longing, despair. Tales of woe. Was there any help? Would anything serve? For anyone? They weren't lost, they were found, by God, and they're all around us. We know them, because they're us. They're us, too. They work on us, they work on our very innards and they become a part of us. Did it ever occur to you what that might do, what it did to us? Scars, injuries we still carry. Was there any going back? Would we ever again be what we'd been before? Could we? At first I saw nothing and didn't think about it. My idea was to try to heal them, of course, heal their wounds. Soothe their dark bruises. Picture that. Repair their fractured souls. Figure it out and try to be there for them, whatever that might mean. Sounds pretty good, right? But it was impossible. Unfortunately.

♦

So a couple of years out of school, I'm in your little clinic and I thought I was lucky. We thought you were good. You shared your gift and we loved you for it. We would never say it in so many words, but that's what it was, a kind of love. Respect anyway. Even now I can put myself back there. I can tell you exactly how you struck us, us pseudo-Romanos. Most of us were in awe. Here was someone who really seemed to know what he was doing. Most of us admired your skills, your way with a patient. That was a big thing. Or maybe it was something else that grabbed us, something we needed. A baby goat or some other critter without a mother bonded with a tin can. Snuggled up to it and felt soothed being close to it. They did an experiment. That's how much all kinds of creatures need to bond with something. Even therapists trying to find their way. And you knew you had us, holding the floor every other Wednesday, you and your self-preening confidence. And why not? We studied you. There was Romano's approach. Romano does this, Romano does that. We could rattle off things you said, your favorite cliches about the personality, what to look for in this or that kind of patient. You had your easy way with people, like a good-natured uncle, or it seemed like that, at least from the outside. You had your own patented brand of chatter. And you'd throw out hints about our cases, therapeutic tidbits, and it sounded right on the money. So you had your gift. Why should I take that away from you? You had your gift and the ripples spread outward. Not that I could do treatment your way. I tried it, but we know I couldn't and can't. And when I came to myself, didn't want to.

♦

And the cases came. God, did they come. There were cases on top of cases. Like I say, those early ones moved me in ways I'll never understand. They struck me right to the core. You had no idea. It was a different world for me. I wonder if any of the others still look back the way I do. I can't help myself.

Remembering for years, going back over things in my mind, going back, loving and cherishing so many moments, but regretting so many more. Bitter, painful regrets. The failures, the failed connections, the chances missed. And missing them, missing them as people, but maybe people I just imagined they were. But missing something about them, something. In all kinds of different ways they entered my life, never to leave me. Like Steven from that first year. Always, always I think back to Steven with his splayed front teeth. He was so nervous and embarrassed to be taking up space on the earth. It wasn't hard to understand. What would anybody feel?

"There was a traumatic incident." He had this detached way of talking about it. "It involved my biological mother. She had been in and out of institutions. She killed herself. It happened when I was nine."

"I'm so sorry. I am so sorry, Steven."

"Yes. It happened in Europe, England. My father was invited to teach. He was a heart doctor. He reacted by being busy with his work. He gave no support in terms of parental involvement. He was strictly old school, so you're not supposed to show any emotions. He told my sisters and me that she had died. That was it. We knew she hadn't been in the hospital or anything."

"I'm so sorry."

"Yes. Nothing more was spoken about it. My mother killed herself Friday night and Monday morning we had to be back in school." Steven looked so calm telling me. It was scary. "My first reaction was to stay close to my father. I was worried. I didn't want anything to happen to him. I didn't want to go to school. And I never knew it was suicide until a year later. My father finally told me."

Steven had one lasting memory of his mother, he told me. She was lying on a bed in a darkened room. "I thought it was a physical thing. But I saw her going down." He told me she had made at least two other attempts.

He said, "I always have the fear something is wrong with me." He was terrified he'd become suicidal himself. He said, "I have suicidal thoughts on a regular basis. I'm afraid I might turn out like her. I worry, what if it happens to me?" He said the thoughts would come but he'd try to stop them. He said, "I try to put them out of my mind, just stop thinking about it." He said he'd gotten better at that. "I realized with me it was just more of a fear. I wasn't going to do anything. I didn't have any real plan." But he was afraid for one of his sisters. He had two older sisters. One of them was troubled and went into therapy, and he would ask the other one, "Do you think Becky is going to kill herself?" And then there was a long period, months, when he was deathly afraid he was being poisoned.

So that was Steven. And there was nothing I could do for him. A fearful, nervous, terrified man. Constantly haunted by suicide and death. He almost couldn't think of anything else.

♦

Do you remember when I came up to your office with my question? You were just getting off the phone and waved me to sit down. I had to clear up something about the whole business. I asked you the question.

"Do you think it helps them even though we don't do anything about their problems?"

"Why do you say we don't do anything? We are doing something."

"What are we doing?"

"You know what we're doing."

"What, just being there and supporting them? So they can center themselves? I know we're supposed to be doing that. But come on. What does that mean, centering themselves? How is that supposed to happen?"

"You know. By clearing away all the rubbish from the past. Focusing on their own needs."

"But how do we know if we're doing that?"

"You're listening, aren't you? Just don't worry about it. You're doing it. This is how it works, Cyril." I didn't say anything. You said it again, "This is how it works."

I said, "Let me think about that." I left. I was lost, and I had already stopped trusting my instincts. When I still thought I had some.

♦

And they kept coming in. Like Beverly, the teacher, I think it was third grade. She said she was caught between an older sister and a younger one. They all lived together. The older one made demands and bullied her and the younger one leaned on her and drained her. She was the doormat. That seemed plain enough and very painful. But I never saw how deep the wounds were that she had. I never got below the surface. Don't ask me why. Even so, I doubt if I could've mended those wounds. A lot of patients would suddenly say things that threw me off. The slim, delicate young guy suddenly railing against the "Bud men" he'd see in a bar. What do you say? Oh, yeah, them, those disgusting types. But I didn't get it right away. He wanted me to be like him. I missed that at first. That had to be what made him quit. So we're supposed to know them right off the bat. We're just like they are and we hope they'll believe us. It wasn't easy and it wasn't automatic. A lot of the time I'd fake it. I'd pretend to understand them and their screwed up stories. You can try to start where they are, but where the hell are they? I didn't know. And so many times they couldn't tell me. So slews of them came and went before I could do anything. Like the teenage kid hooked on heavy metal, and his parents watching him slip away, losing touch with school, friends, his future. He had made up his mind this music was his life, even though he did nothing more than listen to it. He thought vaguely he might buy a guitar. Or the gentle little nine-year-old who couldn't let go of her strange cat obsession. She liked making quick sketches of her favorite animal. She could knock one off in a half a minute. Or the good-

natured, heavy-set plumber with his driving phobia. His wife
had to drive him to work and pick him up later. Or the boy
Pierre, fifteen years old, with his sad, sad, homely face, who
dreaded meeting a couple looking to adopt. He was hopeful and
hopeless at the same time. He knew his chances were slim to
zero. Or the mother with a 22-year-old son who wouldn't see her
or talk with her. He had cut off all contact with no explanation.
This had gone on for six months or more. She was very fragile
and couldn't conceive of any reason for this. It was completely
outside her experience. Or the depressed woman, about 70, who
had moved back to New York from Florida with her husband to
be near her daughter. Then she had regrets. She missed her house
and the life they had down there with their friends. She longed
to go back but she was afraid. Do you think I could ever forget
these people? No, even if they didn't stay I still think of them.
Like the 50-year-old depressed hemophiliac in his wheelchair
who made miniature Shaker furniture, accurate even down the
right kind of wood. This was probably the only thing that kept
him going. He gave me a tiny chair as a memento.

◆

So it's back down in the tunnel, trying to continue. And Lynn
came in. "Now I'm going to cry," she said, first session. And she
did. Then she said, "I've been so depressed." Baffled, blocked,
trying to have a life. This was Lynn, struggling to breathe. She
said, "I live with my mother. But I've been mostly supporting

her for five years. Now she's getting Social Security. It wasn't a big burden. But like, I'm in the living room. I want my own personal space. It's been eating at me. I've talked to friends about it. My situation isn't good."

I said, "It doesn't seem too good."

"No, and my relationships with men haven't lasted, and I wonder if she has anything to do with it."

She paused. Then, "I've had some losses. My grandmother died last fall, my father's mother. I was there in the hospital with her. My uncle also died. We got along well. When my father died, I was away at school, and my mother didn't even tell me he was in the hospital. I came home for the funeral. But even when he was in a coma, I would have liked to be there, you know?"

I said, "Of course."

She went on. "My mother left her job last year, which she didn't warn me about, then she says, 'I can't pay so much on the rent.' Which was okay. I mean, they paid for my college education. But I've paid that back by now. I've basically been paying most of the rent. I think it's time I got out. That's what I think."

I said, "It sounds like you really want that."

"I hate to say it but my mom's gotten to be so selfish. I get home a little late and you'd think she could at least have started the water for spaghetti or something. But I have to do everything. And I do it. I do it because I feel sorry for her. And my brother. He's not a bad person, but he's selfish too. I try to help him. He's been trying to start a driving school. I try to help but he gets all threatened and bent out of shape. He gets sarcastic. 'I think we've more or less covered that subject,' sort of thing. But he's always been that way. He'll ask me to help him, then he'll call me a know-it-all. Like with taxes, for example, which I help him with. I think I'm a good sister to him. And he knows that. I'd like to figure out why he's so negative towards me, especially when I don't do anything. I try not to aggravate him. But then he criticizes me."

I said, "I wonder what it is."

In the next session Lynn was talking about relationships. "I've met a nice person. I met him through a  friend at work. We've started seeing each other. But there's a cultural difference. He's from Egypt. My mother says go meet other people. But this man brings roses, and he asks what he can do for me. I don't know if I should like him or say forget it."

I said, "What do you feel about him?"

She said, "I'm not sure. I know I get nervous with him. That's at work too. Especially when someone male comes into the unit. I sweat and my elbows shake. It's getting worse. It never happened before. And I get nervous when I go out, like to a restaurant, even with a friend. Saturday I got nervous on a date. I made a complete fool of myself because I made up some excuse I had to rush home. I'm sure the guy knew I was lying. And I have fears. My girlfriend found out she was HIV positive and so is another friend of ours. I'm a nervous wreck. I really need to find out why. I don't want to blame my mom, but maybe she's somehow connected. I know I always have guilt when I go out and leave her."

The day after this she called me and said she wasn't going to be able to continue the sessions. She was too busy with obligations at work.

◆

"Hi, me again, your royal pain in the ass." That was Prago, calling me to cancel or something. Maybe you remember. She was the woman who'd been beaten. Prago. Mary Prago. Bay Ridge born and bred. She began a month or two after Lynn. Feisty she made into an art form, always looking for a laugh despite everything. She was beaten coming from a house where she was arranging a funeral. She was a new funeral director and proud she'd arrived. It was just getting dark, and what happens? "These two come from behind the car and beat the shit out of me. I wake up in the hospital," she said. She couldn't work any more or walk easily. She couldn't stand for more than ten minutes. Her pain was constant, with a lot of other aftereffects. She slurred everything and her memory was shot. She had all-day headaches, and on and on. Nightmares, flashbacks, insomnia, tearfulness, hopelessness. I'd listen to her trying to explain something and she'd get lost and wander off the point. Sometimes she'd realize it and laugh at herself. She couldn't stay focused on things she wanted to do, things like the laundry. When she was feeling a little up, she might make prank phone calls. That was her brand of humor. Raucous and raunchy. She should have been able to stay that way. That was her nature. But she'd gotten withdrawn and afraid to leave her apartment. She had fears of break-ins and assaults, even attacks from people in the same building. Some cousin in Florida finally came to the rescue. It was excruciating to see a life laid low and be so helpless to do anything. And she saw it that way too.

♦

I think about Howard, my defeated athlete. You might remember Howard. Huge guy. I saw him as a huge phantom. Impossible to take hold of. The way he talked he seemed hollow. My fault, but I just couldn't see anything going on inside. He'd recite his complaints without feelings. When he came in, he was trying to get into law school, but he knew for a fact it wouldn't work out. He was cursed with bad luck. He said, "It didn't surprise me that instead of getting to go in the fall, now I've got to wait a whole year. But I expect that kind of thing." In college he tried to make the football team. He found it hard, too hard, and he couldn't stop hating himself because he gave up. But he accepted it. He knew he was foredoomed to let himself down, just like he always had. In the practices he didn't sprint fast enough and the coach got on him about it. "He kept saying I wasn't trying, but I was trying, I swear I was." This happened over three or four weeks. He felt humiliated. He quit the team and switched out of the college. He saw himself as a perpetual failure. Defeat was his identity and his destiny. He talked about interviewing for a job, something with the government. He said,

"There's really no chance because that's the way it's always been for me. Things never come easy. I know I won't get it because I don't have enough experience." I asked him, "How can you be so sure?" Howard gave me his thinking. "Because I know that's the way things go for me. And I'm not being a pessimist or anything. I'm really not. I just know how things go for me. They don't work out, at least not right away. I always have to suffer more than other people. And I'm not into self-fulfilling prophesies, but in a way I can predict this. It won't work out because that's the way things go." He almost couldn't wait to regret the future along with the past. He used his job to avoid thinking about anything, present, past or future. He told me, "I've worked the last sixteen days in a row, and I dread the break that's coming up, because there's nothing to do. It's hard." So this was Howard, despairing and isolated. Not that he wept. I felt how he suffered, longing for something or for someone. I felt it from the beginning. I felt it, but I couldn't hear it through all the hollowness. A hollow voice without feeling. Once in a while a feeling would echo out. One day he said, "Sometimes I'm just irritable. I can't put up with people. I give short answers. I don't know if you know what I mean." What should I have done? I know what I should have done. I should have believed in his humanity, Romano. And I should have looked at all his flat words and turned them over so we could both look at them together. And then together we could have taken them up and wrung out all the salt tears.

◆

Remember when I started? It was the same time as Micki. Some character. But so sweet. The fluke how she wound up with us? She told me herself. I guess you knew her father. Anyway, those were difficult days. But they were amazing. I remember them by the weather. It was October. Blustery days when you feel tossed around outside. I used to stand looking out the back and watch the trees blowing. So there I was, and suddenly I'm up to my neck in cases. People pay money for this? I did what I could with whatever I got. Half the time who got what didn't seem to be any great concern of yours. What did you do, flip a coin? Maybe it worked out one way or another, roughly speaking. Very roughly speaking. We'd speak up once in a while. Certain people preferred certain types of cases. Like Denise with the kids. I used to overhear her sessions through the door. I was stupid enough to think I had a feel for it. I didn't. I was busy trying on a role, trying to see myself through your eyes. But the fear, the stark fear. I don't mind telling you they scared me. What was going to happen? When would the craziness break out? They come into the office. They look around. They give my poster a sideways glance, the rosy moonface over the couch. What's that doing here? But for me, how do I make it through the session? And the next one and the next one. It was all confusion and fear, but I thought this must be how you grow. If you survive.

◆

The day we met about the job I was down. I don't know if you sensed it. It was like, now what am I getting myself into? I finished doing something in my apartment and walked over. The air was heavy after the rain the night before. There were wet leaves underfoot. All I remember we talked about was the custody work I'd done. I went on about the interviews, the home visits, reports to the court, the parents fighting over everything. You said something like, "That doesn't sound like much fun." Which it wasn't. I talked about a few cases. There were a lot of alcoholics. Remember that? How sad they were, these guys, they were mostly men, loving their kids but knowing how they failed them. And how helpless they were to make things right. A father who had gone through three or four programs, including Betty Ford, plus years of AA. He'd had a few short periods not drinking, but he still drank and could pass out on occasion. That was all in the record. He'd given up trying to stop. Alcohol was still in control. But he was asking to have his five-year-old son come for day-long visits. He said he could limit himself to a single martini during those days. It was sad. I had another one I told you about, a father who was negotiating with his ex to share custody of their four-year-old daughter. He thought he was entitled to that. It came out he had broken the child's arm. And it happened two different times. Lifting her off the toilet, he said. "I guess I don't know my own strength," was his explanation. All this sort of mind-bending stuff. I remember these other divorced parents, wrangling over their kids. There were three kids, something like five, seven and twelve. I met them. They were nice kids. So the court finally gave the mother custody of all three of them. She won. But after the ruling what does she do? She decides to pick only the five-year-old girl to move with her to Houston. She has a new fiancé and she plans to relocate there with him. She left the two older kids behind in New York where she knew they'd be living with the dad. This was the same man she'd been bashing in court for months, calling him unfit and saying he had abused her and used drugs. So all that kind of thing. Basically what you get are the nastiest fights you can imagine with kids stuck in the middle. And it goes on and on. I didn't tell you much that was uplifting that day. No idea how I came across.

◆

Did we know you, Romano? I didn't know you. The thought makes me a little sick. But so what? We didn't need to know you. Does a patient need to know a therapist? Probably best not to. Remember the time you had some of the group up to your place? We were supposed to meet the notable analyst. I think there were four or five of us. And Evelyn was there. Obviously this was before anything had happened. She laid out some sandwiches. You introduced the visitor, who was an important somebody. She wasn't loud or anything like that, but I thought she was cold. All head, little heart. She spoke carefully and precisely. A smallish woman in grey slacks and horn-rim glasses.

She was dry. Not much juice there. She started by explaining how it was okay to be human with patients and in fact it was quite important to seem real and even to share a little personal information. Imagine that. Personal information no less. If I try to go back, I thought she was sincere but pretty goddamn smug and sure of herself. But it's been years and memories can sour. At that point I guess I wanted to learn from her. Do you remember telling us about your father? The time he came to your friend's house and showed you and your friends how to start a campfire without matches, just with friction on dry wood. You told us he was relaxed and funny and very good with his hands. But you were ashamed because he had a glass eye and you thought he looked freakish. The way you told the story I was moved. It was your openness. You were so natural, telling us all that, about the kind of father you had. And only valued later.

♦

Did you think I got angry? You were right. Things back then, not now. Like why be so blunt, no, actually hurtful, with Jill that day? And about her patient? She had a commitment to him. She really felt for him. She had discussed him before. I guess you weren't listening. This guy had gotten himself into a real bind. His company wanted him to relocate and move to Phoenix. But when he wouldn't move, they let him go. He was a computer expert and he thought he was indispensable. He couldn't believe what had happened to him. He was wounded and shook up. He was fairly bright, but he'd been sadly mistaken. Now he was out of work. But he refused to settle for any of the offers he was getting. He was stuck and he wasn't willing to budge. So Jill's approach starts to come out. I couldn't capture it. I wish I knew more of her thinking. She never talked down to people. She would never throw this man's mistake in his face. She had tact. So imagine how she felt when you barge in and say, "He bagged it, he needs to face that." You hurt her. You should have realized. I won't say you're just intellect because I know you're not. You always said that therapists don't have anything to use except the feelings that they have inside. How could it be otherwise? Jill's eyes filled with tears. She had feelings for this man and she respected him in his pride. Was this some odd new tactic you were throwing at Jill? And at us? It didn't sound like it.

♦

The group gave me more than you did. You wanted it that way. We learned from each other. That was the theory. And we leaned on each other. It was good for a while. Some of the troops could make sense. Megan made sense. We could feel bad about her leg but she didn't. We were all playing some rather serious role or something. This was big stuff. There certainly weren't any Freuds among us. Carl was irritating as hell. Pompous ass, talking with his dry mouth about his favorite people, his lady violinist, and so on. Like anybody cared. I don't know what you thought of her, but I appreciated Micki. She'd wear her tight skirts, trying to be strong, showing off her muscular calves, trying to play up her strong points. She was another pilgrim on the road like the rest of us, not knowing much about herself. But at least she liked the road. And what about the pencils? Somehow Micki had gotten the idea there was something between her and Ed Dow and she had pencils made up with Micki and Ed printed on them. Remember when she presented them to him? Ed laughed out loud. Poor Micki.

♦

But she was no dummy. The way she'd talk about the lore she picked up at her training institute. All this stuff seemed cool, but what did we really know? You remember her two-pronged approach? She said, "There are two things you should always try to line up with the patient. There's the original wound. This is some horrible shock in their life. It could be the parents' divorce, death of a parent, death of a sibling, sick sibling, things like that. The patient has a deep wound from this. The second thing, always look for the way the wound shows up in the therapy. It always will, one way or another." We'd kick these things around. It didn't help much. And then the point about the patient always wanting out of treatment. Micki told us, "From the first minute, the patient doesn't want to be in treatment. Our basic job is to keep the patient in treatment and help them understand why they want to quit. They resist changing. We're trying to make them change and they don't like it. We threaten the status quo."

♦

What help was there? Never mind all the theories. Wasn't it just the simple-minded hope of finding a connection? Connect to that person sitting over there. But how? I had no idea. Aren't we just reaching out in the darkness without knowing the one we touch? And maybe we'll never know them? But think about it. Isn't it sort of miraculous, when it does happen, actually hearing that other person, someone completely different from you? Someone radically other? It took a long time but it started to dawn on me. This can actually happen. Maybe it started that first year. I was puzzled. I knew we didn't have radar. Was there something else, something we couldn't even know? It might not even be something we do. Maybe it just happens, if it ever does. Do we even know when we care? Good question. How do we have feelings for this other soul out there? We feel for them. What does it consist of? What is it, a spark crossing a gap? Our minds might approach not even knowing how. Wind through some trees or something.

♦

I had a weird idea for a while. I once asked you about it. I thought it was easier to know patients when they first came in.

They were more themselves right at the beginning. Things were fresher, more clear. Not quite that simple, but I thought I was definitely onto something. At first you know them for who they are, in those first sessions. Only later something happens. You start to lose them. What was it? Something had to be getting in the way, right? The waters start getting muddied right away. So it must be the treatment itself. They weren't doing it right. They were playing roles, doing impersonations. Or they were shaping themselves to be what I wanted from them. Whatever they thought that was. They wanted to please me. They were shape-shifters. But this wasn't who they really were. And the story was constantly changing. Holes suddenly opening up. Wait a minute, didn't you say such and such last week? Voids, contradictions, you name it. It was beyond me to keep track. They kept getting farther from themselves, trying to be anybody but themselves. Then I was thinking, but don't we all do it? Of course we do. But, no, the real problem was me, losing my focus, getting distracted. I didn't have a clue how to know these people. The truth is, after a while I gave up trying. Who cares who they are? Let's just chug along. But not very happily. When I asked you about it, you naturally repeated all that stuff you liked to tell us. We can't know them at the start, and we can't know them later, and we're so wrong to let them think we know them at all. It's not so much the goal to know them, they should only know themselves. Etc., etc. Tiresome hearing you say it. That couldn't be true, but for a long time I had no idea why.

◆

One I did try to know was Michelle. She came a little later. The young mother. She lasted a while, more than a year. A thousand times more vulnerable than I thought. It was deceptive. She laughed a lot. A nervous laugh. Spritely and petite, a brunette. She had a degree in sociology and she'd been a swimmer in school. With me she'd come out with things she guessed I was thinking, like "You're thinking I was immature, right?" or "You must think that wasn't a good thing to do." At first she talked about her parents. Both bullies. And punitive. The mother was cold as ice. But Michelle was wary. "Let's not get into parent-bashing," she said. "I don't feel right saying critical things about them. I feel I'll lose them if I say negative things. I don't want to feel like they've failed me, because they haven't failed me in many ways." But then more came out. "My mother always keeps me at arm's length," Michelle said. "She never misses a chance to tell me I'm spoiling my daughter. And she'll yell at me, like if Jessie slips and falls down." Her father was worse. He teased her, calling her his little butterball. He dominated everyone in the family. "I'm afraid of him," she said. "I'm afraid he'll get angry. I remember when I was little I knocked over my milk at the table. He came after me really angry and spanked me and sent me to my room. When I was an adolescent I felt uncomfortable with him. Like hugging him. I'd feel his penis. I was afraid to pull away. Or when he'd linger in my room, five or ten minutes. Enough already." One week she was saying how he made her feel stupid. "He called again, asking if I'd sent him back a paper he needed me to sign. He had sent it for me to sign. So last week I couldn't find it. Finally, I located it and went ahead and Fed Exed it. But when he called I of course got all flustered. He kept asking, did you send it Fed Ex, did you send it Fed Ex? And I said, I called your office and got your Fed Ex number and sent it. And he said, 'Then you did send it Fed Ex!' Like that. That's what I mean. He makes me feel like a flake. And he'll make me feel stupid about money. He'll say things like, 'You're worried about Jessica's school picnic and I'm talking about enough to put the kid through Yale.'" A lot of what Michelle talked about was feeling cheated, never getting what her sisters got. "I had to give up things being the youngest. Like the vacations. I felt like I was being punished. I was lonely. I felt abandoned. I had to stay behind with my grandmother. She used to put me to bed with a candy bar." So Michelle wound up putting everyone's needs ahead of her own. She said, "I know I try to do too much for everyone. I do it with my parents, my sisters, teachers. I really just don't want to disappoint anybody. I think that's one of the reasons I wanted to go into therapy, to focus on myself, because this is the one place just for me." But when she was taking a class, she couldn't ask for an extension to write a paper. "I don't want the teacher to think I'm not serious. I'm feeling a lot of anxiety about it. I don't know why. But I'm always that way. I've been working in my neighbor's apartment, just to get away. I need to isolate myself. I have my laptop there. But you know what the problem is? If I could just lower my standards for just this one thing. But I can never seem to do that. I can never lower my standards." I asked her about that. "It goes back to my father, I guess. And my mother. That I'll let them down, that I won't be a good girl. I don't want to let anybody down." And the whole thing came into the therapy. She didn't want to disappoint me. She said she felt bad calling and rescheduling. "I didn't want to put you to any inconvenience because I'd already rescheduled those other two sessions. But I had things piling up, taking care of Jessie, meetings at the school. Plus writing my term paper." Or when she completely missed a session, the embarrassment she felt. "I feel bad. I hate messing up like that, I really do, and I had all this stuff I wanted to talk about." Or when she began a session with, "I almost didn't want to come here today. I need the extra time for myself. But I'm here." Or when she ended a session saying, "I feel I have to rush away when the time's up. I don't want to take up your time." Everyone else in the universe before Michelle.

♦

I told myself I was learning. And some cases actually seemed to go pretty well once they were moving. I used to wonder what you would have done with Phil Whitaker? He came in for almost six months. You never said anything. It was about his failed marriage. Phil didn't hold back. "What did I do to make her fall out of love with me? What did I do? My wife lost all desire for me." He wasn't past it four years later. I brought him up in the group a couple of times. Megan suggested couples therapy, but they had tried that, back where they were living, north of Pittsburgh. Phil's ex-wife was from that area. Now Phil was back in New York without her and he agonized. "Carrie was exactly what I wanted and I blew it. She was beautiful and down-to-earth. She was the perfect woman for me and I blew it." You learn how repetitive people can be. "I really miss her. I even think a part of me enjoys this. It's like I enjoy feeling rejected. I seem to like the romantic image of myself with a broken heart. There I am alone in the bar, with a glass of scotch in front of me, feeling sorry for myself. That's good for about an hour. But this has become a way of life for me. I get up in the morning and start in saying what a messed up life I've got. I get busy and forget it during the day, but I get my blues back at night." So he kept whipping himself. He was a weakling, a wimp, a loser. He went over and over his missteps. He never asserted himself, never showed his wife who was boss, the way a real man would. Then there was the buddy he had out there where they were living, an old coot he hung out with. Kind of a backwoodsman, totally self-sufficient. He built his own house from odds and ends and scraps of lumber. He became something to aspire to. He wasn't taking any crap off anybody. Phil said he tried the same tack with Carrie, telling her off about different things. Which didn't help. I imagine it left her completely baffled, hearing this from Phil as if from a parrot. He let me know he was good at a lot of things, like his construction skills.

And he played the guitar. He said Carrie loved all this and she loved him. With a passion. Until she didn't.

◆

I suppose I did my job. I listened to Phil kicking himself. "I'm just too weak. I'm insipid. I'm really pathetic." The sessions went along. As I said, they were very repetitive. He saw that. "I haven't had any new thoughts. I'm still in my state of frustration." At some point he took a different slant. I remember feeling relieved. He sounded a little different. It was close to the end. It sounded like he was easing up on himself and being more practical.

He said, "I've been operating on a desire to control. It looked like a desire to help."

"What do you mean?"

He said, "I was always trying to help Carrie with some problem. I was always stepping in to help. But what I really wanted to do was make her see me as a savior. It put me up there. I was the hero."

I said, "Interesting. Did it work?"

He said, "Yeah, it did, a little. But I need to find my real strengths."

He started going to karate classes. He said it was teaching him how to be independent. His teacher told him it wasn't so important to beat an opponent but to use the opponent to learn about yourself. Phil liked that. So for a while he talked about feeling stronger. He realized he didn't have to think about Carrie at all if he didn't choose to. He said, "I'm trying not to think about her, and I don't call. I don't even want to. I miss her but I just can't keep thinking about it. Also, I'm not feeling so responsible for her." He kept busy with his job and his karate and watching football with people at work. For a month he seemed different.

♦

Then he surprised me. Carrie was in from out of town and she was in the waiting room. Would I talk to her? Of course. He thought this would dramatize the situation for me and help me see it better. Why not? So she comes in, Phil waiting outside. She's quite beautiful, just like Phil said. She's wearing a little western vest and an ankle-length denim skirt. And the young woman could talk and she knew herself. She said, "I fell out of love. I married too young. I outgrew Phil. Now I just want to help him get past it and move on." Okay. That sounded good. So let Phil's stuckness be established. Now what to do. Was he getting any better, she wondered. What could I tell her? I guessed he was improving. I said he was working on it. So she left. But look at it, Romano. Yes, his grief was real and he wanted sympathy. But a lot of his talk was just to show himself in a good light. That became his main project. And I let it happen. He would tell me how his wife had admired him, how dramatic his loss was. He would show me how he could let loose and put himself down. Even the karate was something to brag about. Now he was showing me the actual, real live woman he'd gotten to fall in love with him, and it looked like that was going to be enough. He didn't continue long after that. In all those months was there anything that brought on tears or moved our hearts? Was there even anything real, anything that we could lay our hands on? We never got any traction. I doubt if any of it helped him. Half the time he was sitting there smiling at my caring.

At some point a different shade or tone. Things were changing. Something was happening with me. It wasn't clear. Maybe something with my people. Something was going on. That second winter it got intense. I'd walk in the snow down to the office, lost in feelings. Which one was it, or was it only one in particular? Maybe all of them. The same old questions, where did I go wrong, how did I go wrong? I'd turn it against myself. Man, the trouble you can make for yourself. And I did. I put myself through it. So there were these changes in me. It would have helped if you had let me know just a little more how I was doing. I have to say it. Anything to give me an idea of what to do or where I was at. But then how would I have taken it? I'm proud, so I don't know. What if you had bothered to take the trouble and say something? Try this, Cyril, or you might try that. I might have just told you to save your breath. It's a dead issue now, of course. It's been dead this long, long while. I've already said that. I don't know why I keep dwelling on it.

♦

I had so many feelings about people I saw. I'm sure everyone feels this. So many moved me. Like I'm crossing a street and I look back and a little kid is running across to get to his mother who's already on the curb and he loses his sneaker and he sees the cars bearing down and I see the terror on his face. Or once I was on the subway at one end of a car and I heard a thump from the other end and I looked up and saw a large man sprawled on the floor. I go over there and help him onto a seat. He's drunk and his glasses have flown off onto the floor a couple of feet away. I give them to him. He tries to make a joke about some politician in the news. A young woman stands up and seems concerned. She asks him if he's all right. The other passengers are not getting involved, looking anywhere but at the man who'd fallen down. I asked him where he had to go and got off with him to wait for his train. Just to make sure he didn't stumble onto the tracks. He told me about his Army service and showed me his ID card. He had his pride after all. And I remember a lot of other things. This was a long time before I even thought about doing therapy. I had shocks, harsh shocks. Like I'm living on the Lower East Side and these homeless men would come inside the building and sleep under the stairs. It was pathetic and pitiable. Plus frightening. And one of them died there one winter night. Horrible, horrible thing, and no one thought about it for more than a second and a half. I was talking to a cop who was there. He said something like, "Ahh, most of them are healthier than we are." Or the time I happened to sit near this stinking, dirty, drunk, disheveled woman on one of the benches in the middle of Broadway in the seventies. She was whipped. I asked her if she needed any help. She told me where she lived. I managed to get her into a cab and take her home, a walk-up only a few blocks away. She pointed to the apartment and I knocked on the door. A stocky man in an undershirt appeared and brought her inside. He muttered, "Come on in, you dirty rat."

◆

What answers? None probably. I thought I was working my way. There was one thing. It must have been the pity. It was not just feeling bad for them but feeling the pity. Stabs of pity for them in their anguish. You told me pure pity does nothing. That was you. Coming from how you worked, how you grew up, who knows what. I had no idea. It was just you, how you were made. And then you liked to say people don't change, the most they can hope for is some self-awareness. My thing was different. Because if they get some awareness of themselves, why can't they change? Maybe a little at a time. It might even start with a little pity for themselves. That's a change, isn't it? And it will grow. Pity opens our hearts, Romano. That's what it does. That's what it's for. Then we can feel the anguish, the anguish all around us, and stop being dead to it. Instead of pity you might call it love and you'd be right. Love and pity. Pity and love. I thought they were wrapped up with each other. I wasn't sure how it worked. But pity along with love was definitely the driving force. It had to be. What we needed inside to keep us going. I floundered around. I didn't understand it. But I knew we needed to love. We need to love, much more than we need to be loved. And then I started to feel, why do we have to be so goddamned premeditated? We can't be so detached all the time. Like all of us, they're in some sort of pain. We won't be able to help them unless we first hear the pain. Whether they cry out with it in their throats.

◆

Man comes in, desperately needs support. Jim Greer. I know you remember him. His wife has been pushing him to get help, so here he is. Why didn't she want help for herself? I don't know. Maybe she was seeing someone already. They have one child, a 17-year-old daughter. Sally has cancer, brain cancer. She's getting chemotherapy at Columbia Presbyterian. It's been three months and it's working. The cancer is arrested, it's stable. Jim says, "Her doctor is a really wonderful man. He's handled Sally from the beginning. Sally loves him. I think she has a crush on him," Jim says. He tries to laugh. We've only had about four sessions. Of course, things change. Jim tells me they've found signs that the  cancer has spread and they've found it in her lungs. By the next session, it has spread further. He and his wife are beside themselves. Jim has the guts to come in for a final session to tell me that they're without hope, they're going to lose her. "She's so brave," he says. "She's my hero," and he breaks down, sobbing. And I'm stupidly, stupidly silent, with no idea how to say anything to him. I lean over and grip his hand with both of mine, and we hug a long couple of minutes at the door. And a day later I'm trying to tell the group, and Dani has to take me out of the room.

♦

You loved telling us about your theory. Yes, the sacred theory. I'm afraid you wanted us to be a lot more theoretical than we were. I started to resent it, always pushing those ideas of yours. Like each person's head is a private universe. A cosmos of its own, available only to the owner. I have an idea why you might believe something like that. But it can't be true. Thinking we're always unknown to each other is absurd. Isn't it obvious we have to try to know people? That should be on page one, and I've said as much. We should have hashed it out a long time ago. Along with so many other things. Because knowing people is everything. Otherwise what are we doing? And we have to believe we can do it. I mean know them intimately. Try to know people and know their pain. I was barely getting a glimmer of it. And it was painful work, for me it was, because along with it you're opening yourself. And, let's face it, I never got good at it, but they might sense I was trying. Then by their talking to me and my talking to them, I started to feel there was a chance. Maybe we could find the healing words. And once the pain is named and covered with words, it doesn't hurt so much. Unless you just don't make the connection and you stay strangers. No connection. That's always a possibility and it happened to us more than any of us wanted to admit. But it was never like your private universes. You have to think about human pain, and the way it hits each of us, with its different strengths and tones and undertones. My pain has to be radically different from yours. But whatever it is, pain is the main thing that binds us together. Misery loves company. You never believed in something like that. I always wondered about you, the isolationist. It must feel very lonely.

♦

So many failed connections. Which were my fault. Like the one with Helene. Graceful, soft-spoken Helene, who'd been through her accident. It must have been during the time I was seeing Phil. It wasn't good. She had broken some bones in her face. It had all healed completely and there was no trace of the accident. No outward trace. She had great color to her face and big, dark eyes. She didn't feel the same, though. She couldn't even put into words what she wanted from me. She said over and over, "It was just a terrible shock." She'd lost herself in the accident. She didn't know it. I didn't either. Her need was to get herself back. I didn't realize it until later, and by then it was too late. And anyway, how would she manage to do that, to get herself back? How would you talk to her about it? She looked so healthy, and she had a beautiful aura about her. I still see her elegant, smooth face. But for her this wasn't Helene anymore. She didn't quite feel she was there. She sensed something was wrong, something was absent. Or let's just call it a weakness in the way she saw herself, something she needed to build up. But I lost her very quickly. I felt like there was a precious thread that was starting to connect us. One day I broke it. She was sitting on the couch and quietly looking at me. I happened to look away from her. I remember I reached over and moved a book lying on my desk so I could read the title. Why would I do that? That was enough to break our connection. She stopped coming.

♦

But you keep trying. A few of them might have been funny if they hadn't been so very sad. Like that couple Ginnie and Rob. Right away you get the definite vibe there's something mighty strange going on. I couldn't tell exactly what. The two of them came in and I was thinking they should be fighting and arguing about something. Isn't that why couples come to therapy? But that didn't happen. Nothing was happening, so what was it with these two? They were comfortable with each other. They were tender with each other. They talked about their long relationship. They talked about their travels together. Chitchat like that. They'd spent time in England and other places. They talked about rearranging Rob's apartment. They had changes to make before Ginnie could move in. They had to change the shower, I think. There had to be a separate shower stall or something. I forget the details. There was no big money problem. Rob was accommodating about everything. They were extremely sweet with one another. Then one week they come in and Ginnie drops the bomb.

"I've told Rob the truth. I'm not attracted to him."

"Oh? Have you talked about this?"

"She told me last night."

"Did you have any idea?"

"No, not really. It's a surprise but what can I do? If it's the fact, I guess that's that. There's nothing I can do about it." And Ginnie was nodding. She was as resigned to it as Rob was.

So. This sudden change. I never saw it coming. It was so low-key. No voices raised, no tears. They accept it, just like that. They both regret it, but it's presented as a given. It just happens to be coming to light. They could have seen it before but now that they see it, it's no big deal. Rob isn't shocked, mad or sad, and that was the oddest part. And to me the saddest. But he's cool, and Ginnie is completely matter-of-fact. You'd guess there was another man in the wings. There was no mention of one. She was saving Rob the hurt. They cared for each other. But wait. That's right. There were a couple of weeks there when they didn't come in. Ginnie had a short vacation by herself. She flew to London and did some shopping. Did something happen there? Who knows? Maybe just her revelation. No attraction. None at all. That's all there was to say. And now, it's sad regrets all around but Ginnie's feelings are Ginnie's feelings. So a month later I get a note from Rob. He thanked me for my help. He said I'd made the meetings productive.

♦

And what about the confessers? I got a few. They had just one main thing on their minds they had to tell me. When they got that done, they left. Remember Defries? He was that tough-looking, strong-looking guy who'd swagger into the building. He looked both ways before he came into my office, like he was crossing a street. He wore denim shirts and jeans. He was well-informed and he liked politics. He had his lefty positions and he talked about them with a lot of conviction. In his second session, which turned out to be his last, he came out with the fact that he sometimes put on women's underwear. I remember his poor eye-contact. He never came back. Confession could have been why Felicia came too. Or maybe she was just an exhibitionist. She was young and attractive. She was a one-timer. She said her parents' separation was on her mind a lot. Her father had left the family. He was from the mideast, I think she said. She was working as a bartender on the East Side. She said the place catered to a young crowd and on weekends when things were fun and exciting she'd pull up her shirt and flash her bare breasts for the crowd. She smiled and said it was just for kicks.

♦

Dreams people had? You never lingered over them, but somehow they figured into your theory. I didn't quite get it. What was it? There's the dream life the person has and the waking life going on at the same time. There's a close connection. They join with each other. Isn't that pretty obvious? When one isn't happening, the other takes over. Anyway, I didn't even think about it. If a patient brought in a dream, I'd plunge right in. A tall, dashing fellow is riding along the seashore on a magnificent white horse. The horse's mane and tail are just flowing back in the breeze. It was like slow motion. It's a sunny day in a beautiful place. So then the horse and rider start moving off the beach and into the shallow water, when suddenly a sniper starts shooting at them. This is a deadly surprise. The horse gets hit and goes down. The white of the horse gets stained red. It's bleeding into the water. The rider manages to make it to the shore and escapes the danger. That's the end. My architect Ray came in with this one. I think you knew about him. Ray was my dreamer par excellence. That shy, non-assertive man. He worked for a company, but needed to pass a final exam to get his license. He failed it over and over, and always because of some small mistake, which he'd kick himself about afterwards. He'd say, "I just can't believe I missed that." There was always some catch to a question that caught him by surprise. It caused him such pain. It was probably in his last session he told me the horse dream. I still remember his shy smile telling it. He was enjoying this one. The setting struck me later. No buildings! No design problems to solve! Was that important? Anyway, let's say Ray started the dream as the magnificent horse rider. So he must feel pretty good about himself. But some inner fear starts the sniping. Ray and I never understood it. Was it all about the tricky exam questions? I told him what I thought. The dream might be saying, Ray, if you want to escape danger and save yourself, give up the magnificent white horse and use your own legs. In other words, give up on the exam. It's killing you. Or then again maybe don't give up. The dream might be telling you, yes, you're afraid of the exam but you'll survive it one way or another, maybe not in grand style, but you'll do it. Or maybe it wasn't about the exam at all. In another dream Ray breaks into a bakery at night. He wants to get some black and white cookies. But someone surprises him there. There's a woman behind the counter. She's someone he knows, a friend of his mother's. Neither of us had any idea what that was about. Sometimes they were grotesque. Like this one. Ray sees these huge metal cables that are twisting and writhing and very hot. He realizes they're actually the coils of an enormous snake, intertwined with itself. Then he sees there's a person growing out of the coils at one end. It's a man, the head and arms and chest of a man. He's dressed in a black suit with a white shirt and a black tie. But the lower part of the man is all snake. Then Ray sees a woman walking near there, he's not sure who she is. He runs to where she is and warns her to stay away, because of the snake man. Then he has to leave her and come back to where he was. Now he sees the snake man stabbing a dog, a brown dog, and he's stabbing it in the back. He's offering pieces of the dog to a woman. It's the same woman Ray had warned to stay away. She has come back. And she's actually eating pieces of the dog. She's been corrupted. Ray said that was the worst part. He said his own moaning woke him up. We didn't know what to make of it. Who was the snake man, who was the dog, who was the woman? Did it remind him of anything? He didn't know. He said one time he was driving with his girlfriend in the car with him, and they went past a building he had designed, a big warehouse. He pointed it out and she said, "That doesn't look very hard to do." Could she be the woman in the dream? Ray couldn't decide.

♦

"There's no marriage." The wife Suzanne started with this and went on. "There's nothing between us.   Nothing." You remember the Reynaldos, Suzanne and Pete? Another couple that first year. For arguing they didn't disappoint. I always remember them as the Car Wash Couple. They owned one in New Jersey.

I asked Suzanne, "No marriage?"

"No."

"Do you love each other?"

"Yes."

"Do you agree with that, Pete?"

"Yes, I love her."

"Anybody see a contradiction? Two people, married, and love each other, yet there's no marriage?"

Pete said, "I love her, but I think she's been kind of depressed toward me since Noel left." This was their youngest son, in his 20s, living in California.

I asked him, "What does she do?"

"She hasn't been talking to me very much."

"And you think it's because she's depressed about Noel leaving?"

"I think so."

"Could you ask her if that's what's been going on?"

"What do you mean?" Pete asked.

"I mean, could you ask Suzanne directly if she hasn't been talking to you because of Noel?"

Pete looked at her. "Is there something about Noel that's the reason you're quiet towards me?"

Suzanne said, "We do miss him. I was sad about Noel. Very sad. I'm sad he went but that's over. We just have nothing to talk about. Pete is mostly interested in his things. He's not interested in talking to me about them. We keep to ourselves. We don't ever talk."

I said, "I can believe it. You notice how neither of you speaks directly to the other one? You speak mostly to me."

And Suzanne said, "Yes, I was going to say that. Why do we talk to you in here? We should be talking to each other."

And Pete said, "It's because she's so negative. I can't stand hearing it. She's always correcting me. The least little thing."

I asked, "Could you give me an example?"

"Sure. Like the car wash. I decided to lower the price to get more business. And I did and luckily business picked up a little on the weekend. But she had something to say, like, So what."

Suzanne said, "Here's actually what happened. I told Pete that since there's a car wash near ours that not only gives a wash but also gives a real full-service cleaning, inside and out, for the same price as he gets for just the wash, why would people pay the same for less service? Why would they come to him?  I told him this months ago, maybe a year ago. Because he's losing business to the other wash."

Pete said, "No.  It isn't a matter of service. It's territory. People nearby will come to me. And they do. They will. It was a business decision to bring the price down for the time being. That was my decision." Suzanne was shaking her head.

Pete said, "I don't mind it so much her trying to help with the business. She has some good ideas. But there are a lot of other things."

I said, "Like what other things?"

"Like her telling me I was driving to Brooklyn the wrong way."

Suzanne said, "No, it was just that my way was the one they all said was better. Not through all the traffic. It wasn't a criticism."

I said, "But Pete, you heard it as a criticism?"

"Yeah, definitely. Who wants to hear it?"

And Suzanne, "Well, he doesn't have to put me down all the time."

Pete said, "I don't think I do that."

And Suzanne, "He humiliates me in front of people. Like here's a good example. One of my friends had just lost her mother and we were talking in the kitchen and he comes home and walks in and looks around and says, 'Are we going to eat?'"
And Pete, "I just came home. I didn't know what was going on. I wondered if we were eating or not."
And Suzanne, "A terrible thing to say. It was so cruel. It was so humiliating. My friend and I just looked at each other."
"I just came home," Pete said. "What did I see?"
"You know, he doesn't do this with other people. Just me."
They could go on and on in this vein. They talked endlessly about not talking, about Pete retreating to the TV room and Suzanne keeping to herself in the bedroom. She said, "We're probably one of the few families with no TV in the living room. It's just as well. We don't like to watch the same things."
Obviously that one went nowhere. We never got beyond all the asinine bickering.

♦

How were we supposed to keep going? No one talked about it. How did the others cope? You're constantly afraid you'll go under. Tim reached out at one point. He had his own private despair, but you'd never know it, quiet as he was. He was looking for some kind of support. Why would he think I could help? For all he knew I might have been as lost as he was. Which I was. He never seemed that comfortable in the group. We should have tuned in to him better. I feel bad about it. He was sort of a bookish type. Maybe you remember? Maybe not. It could have been during one of your periods of distraction. But Tim was a good person. He and I used to talk. I can still see his stubble, brown eyes, the green-and-black checked shirt he'd wear around the clinic. He had me over for dinner one night. This was a nice gesture. They were on East 93rd. A big old apartment with faux wood-paneling and bookshelves everywhere. Nan was more relaxed than Tim. We drank a lot of beer, not Nan, just Tim and I.

At one point Tim was asking me something. "Could we trade notes on patients? Some of them are so confusing. I don't know. It'd be nice to trade notes on some of them. What do you think?"

"Tim. I think that's a great idea."

He said, "I'm not doing too well. I'm not sure what to do with a couple of them."

"So let's trade notes. Let's do it."

It got late and I remember I was trying to tell him there's always something better than suicide. "Tim," I was saying. "There's always another way. Always. Even if you go to the South Seas or somewhere and help the natives."

I woke up in a spare room. I was on top of the bedding with a heavy blanket thrown over me. Nan was going over my face with a wet washcloth. She was very gentle. "Good morning, Cyril." I was embarrassed and still beery. Nan wasn't disgusted. I had to wonder about Nan. She seemed almost happy that I was hung over and had gotten drunk with her husband and collapsed. What was it? I felt like I'd been recruited into the couple. Tim was in trouble and Nan was going to help him in whatever way she could. But I never really got to know him. He quit two months after that and we never got to trade notes on any cases.

♦

One day Manny was giving us an update on one of his people. I'm sitting there and I can't believe what I'm hearing. The thing is, you were reinforcing everything, you were so pleased at the wonderful support Manny was giving this patient. She was a young woman. She had all kinds of insecurity about herself. You know the one I mean? Bobbie, Roberta. Manny is aware of all her doubts about herself and he's telling us about them. Is this the person you and Manny feel so good about? She didn't know how she felt as a wife. A lot of days she felt she wanted a divorce. She hated the way she looked. Serious stuff. But it sounded like this wasn't important to Manny or you. It's like you were both saying Bobbie and her marriage would be just fine as long as she kept striking the right poses, acting like everything was right and normal. But to me Bobbie and her husband act like a couple of plastic mannequins. Going through their paces. They seem to get along, she takes care of the apartment, cooks excellent dinners, really loves to cook, they're having regular sex, etc., etc. But Bobbie was shaky inside. That's what I'm hearing. Very shaky. Almost on the brink. She doesn't feel like the model spouse. She thinks she should feel it, but she doesn't feel it. And Manny is there applauding the role she's playing. And you're telling Manny he's doing just the right thing with her. So what's going on? Is this the way to operate? You give us your cliche. "Bobbie has resources that will come out and renew her and help her get centered. But she needs Manny's approval and support through the process." I have to say something. "Manny. With all due respect, you're not getting Bobbie at all. I doubt if your therapy is helping at all. Isn't she really in trouble?" And Manny says, "I don't think so. I think she's doing okay." And you say, "The main point is Manny's support. And Bobbie knowing it's there." I say, "Support what? Don't you people see she's in pain? It's horrible. She's crying for help." No one wanted to say anything. I say, "Is it that hard to hear the pain she's in? Are we afraid of it?" The group knew what I was getting at.

♦

You know who comes to mind? Ann McGrath. Here was pain. She was isolated, unloved, and in a lot of pain. But she was so muted and muffled. And wooden and stiff. Poor stiff Ann. Six months she was with me. Tall, always in jeans, awkward, with her severe face and dull hair. And her flat, flat voice. She came from a rural area. I don't remember what brought her to New York. She worked in a home for disabled kids. There was no husband or partner I ever heard about, but she had a son in a private school in New Jersey. She certainly cared about him. She said she felt out of place among the other parents. I doubt if there was anywhere Ann didn't feel out of place. One day out of the blue she starts talking about her father.

"He was cruel. That's all, just cruel."

"How was he cruel?"

"He hit me. He hit me a lot. After a while I didn't talk to him. I stopped talking in the house."

No more expressive than that. Another time she said, "My parents fought. It scared me. I didn't know why, and I used to think I was the reason."

There were a couple of months like this and then she told me about her suicide attempt as a kid. Just a young kid! Impossible to get your mind around. One night she crept out of the house and tried to drown herself in a creek at the end of the yard. Ghastly! I sat speechless. Just a young kid. Think about it. Her face was stony telling me. Only this once did I see her eyes get moist. At least that. Everything about Ann was so hard and cold and barren and lonely. Telling me about that awful night in the driest, flattest voice you can imagine. I did notice that her voice thickened as she talked about it. You know what I started feeling? I was completely wrong to feel it. But I thought Ann was close to becoming just a thing to herself, as terrible as that sounds. The woman almost seemed like a hard, unfeeling thing. Which was how her father had treated her.

♦

I thought it was me. I was getting droves of the depressed, one after another, like an epidemic. And your heart goes out. I think of Raia. How washed out she always looked, so pale and exhausted. She was an absolute dishrag. Her 10-year-old son was autistic and it wiped her out. Unending effort with so little in return. I couldn't imagine. But she tried to sound bright and alive. It was a strain. In a thin voice she'd be trying to tell me about some modern painter she liked or some psychology guru. I would join in and try to flatter her for being on top of all those things. You try to be supportive but it was a weak support. It was useless. Didn't give her anything she needed. I'm sinking down while I think about it. I can't bring Raia's face to mind exactly. Pale and puffy, I picture it, and blotchy when she got sad and tearful. So much intelligence, but a lot of good it did her. And there I was echoing her own interests back to her. Bad way to go. Taking it away from her. I was hearing the wrong Raia, the bright one, not the sad one. It couldn't have made her feel one iota better. But who knows?

♦

Then I get my sad, comely Barnard student. Would you hold back, like I did? I had to protect her and I had to protect myself. This was a tender person, Debora. Soft dark hair, so gentle, her small hands. The delicate ways she had. Speaking with one hand cradling another. Half Swedish, half American Jewish. Mother hadn't been with her for years. She'd lived always with her father, who was on Wall Street. I think she was having trouble with school when we started. I mostly remember the loneliness. Her endless loneliness. I pictured her walking the long, carpeted corridors in a big Westchester house, dark and silent. She haunts the upper corridors. I don't know if she said that or if I filled it in. She was so quiet a person, the whole picture was one of quiet. Someone had turned the sound off. At that point I kept her to myself. I had to. I wasn't comfortable with someone this delicate. How could I risk people trampling all over her? That could easily happen in the group. But after a month I realized I could use some help. Some of the group would see her tenderness and her loneliness. They'd get her, and maybe you would, too. Big mistake.

You started in. "She's not going to break into pieces. Address her reality and where she is developmentally. She's always had the one main object in her life, her father. That's what she needs to look at." That was the gist, setting me straight, with all the stages and whatnot.

And I say, "No. That's not it at all. Debora's a whole person apart from her father. She's lonely and lost. And her father won't help her, he never has, so it's senseless to bring him into it." I couldn't sit still for all your clinical palaver.

You said, "Well, Cyril. What's this all about?"

"What's it about? It's about this fragile person I'm trying to help. That's what it's about. She has suicidal thoughts, too. Which she's very stoical about, by the way."

"How come you didn't mention that?"

"And you know what she said to me last week? She was looking straight at me and she asked, just so openly, 'What is that feeling? You feel okay. Things are okay. I've had it a few times, when you feel different, you don't think of sadness very much, you don't feel so bad?' I'm telling you that's exactly what she said."

I think you stood up.  Your eyes said nothing.

♦

One morning I got a note in my box, "Need to see you about an urgent case." I went up to your office and the door was open. So we had our back and forth. I remember at first you didn't say a word. You picked up the intake that was on your desk and handed it to me. It turned out to be Treanor. I looked at the file and said something like thanks or I'll start it.

Then your question, "Don't you think we're doing enough, Cyril?" Was this a real question? Or was it about Debora?

"What do you mean?"

"I don't know. I get the feeling you think we don't do enough for the people who come in. I wonder about it myself."

I didn't say anything. I guess I mumbled, "Uh-huh." Then, "They're difficult. We get very sad cases."

"Anyway, how are you? We don't get to talk."

I said, "I'm okay." I was looking down at the file I was holding. I was wondering what you were getting at.

"Anyway, come and talk. I'm here. Talk to me. About a case or anything. Anything you want to talk about. Okay?"

I said, "Thanks." Then, "You say we should talk, you know, but I've got to be honest. I'm not sure I believe you. I hate to say it, but I get the feeling you're not really interested."

"What? Of course I am. I'm interested in you and your work, just like with everyone's."

"Well, it doesn't always feel that way. You might be preoccupied. I realize that."

"Of course I'm interested."

"I talk and it feels like you're indifferent. And some of these people have been through the worst horrors and things that would break your heart."

"I don't know what to say. You know I take an interest in everything that comes to my attention."

"Well, there've been different ones. Like Steven Keyes. What did you tell me? You said, don't worry about it, he'll be okay. You didn't care."

"I don't remember that."

I said, "You're distracted. That's how you come across."

I remember you said, "I don't think so," and then something like, "To be continued, Cyril, when we have more time."

♦

Then the unfortunate drama in your office and I was trying to talk. I'm having a hard time getting it out. I'm nervous. I'm hearing myself fumbling words and stumbling all over the place. I'm trying to explain it to you. "Romano, we have to realize, so

many are lost in their own dark caves. They're lost. They can't
see any light or maybe they see a little but they haven't reached it
yet. They're trying to reach the light. You understand? We have
to help them. We can't be throwing out obstacles, blocking the
light. We can't block the light with all our stuff. And they cry
out with things, out of the depths. They cry out. They're crying
out to be heard. We have to try to hear their cries. Quiet cries
that are in there somewhere, beneath or between the words.
We've got to hear them, Romano. Their cries of pain. Or maybe
just the echoes. That might be all we can hear. But be as close as
possible. Hear their voices echoing out. Try to be a listener."
That's what I needed to tell you. I might have used better words.
I know that. I just wanted to get through to you. I know you
didn't expect anything of this nature. But after I stopped, then
your words. More than wounding. "I don't believe this. What is
all this bullshit? What the hell is the matter with you, Cyril?
Have you lost your mind?" And then you slam the book shut
that you had on your desk. Slamming me shut.

♦

How was I the week after that? How were you? Things happen
and can't be helped. They cast shadows over the heart. Some
things can never be undone, only forgotten. That I've learned.
But why be insulting? Why? You acted like the worst sort of
narrow bullying fascist. With a little effort you could have
understood. Whether you agreed or not. It was obviously

important to me. But, of course, you weren't open. Was it just your pride? Because I wasn't like you? I know you needed your followers. I was letting you down because of who I'd become. What can I say? People change. I wasn't what you expected. But then another thing I realized. I wasn't hearing you, even you, for who you were. You had every right to be in your own framework, the one you'd built up around yourself. So I wasn't hearing your cries, your own cries. So I failed myself as well as you. I failed even on my own terms. And that hurts, that hurts. And I don't seem to have the kind of brain that can put things away in that dim space where they may or may not be brought to light. It's a curse, not to forget. Your insults that day entered the living archive. Your words stabbed right into me. You should know that.

♦

Give me this at least, I tried to tell you. My thing about listening to patients in a different way. Try to hear people differently? Is that so hard? That was the beginning. That's what we had to do or at least try to do. That was the main point, the only point, really. That and the fact that they couldn't put these feelings, all this pain, into words. It's not in the words. So try to listen beyond the words. It's distant. It's early stuff. It's made out of the simplest elements. The simplest emotions. Feelings and hurts and shocks. The quiet, almost silent twists of the heart that words don't even exist for. Songs and quiet moans made out of sighs and whispers and wails and whatever else. It's all pieces and shards and shreds. It's all in there among the words if we can hear it. The thing is, I thought we should come and wait nearby. I thought we were privileged that way. We were the watchful, the hopeful, waiting in the night air, if you will, close to them in their caves. But listen, always listen for the cries no one hears, the cries under the words, the things we didn't know were there, the cries of pain you said I made up. And I know damn well it takes a much better ear than I have, and a much better heart, to always hear it, to listen for it and always hear it. That weak, helpless sound coming from so far away. It's nearly extinguished by its own utterance. It's unmistakable when you hear it. Because you're hearing something in yourself. When did I realize that? I don't know when, but you didn't want to understand. You can imagine that hasn't led my spirit towards any peace. And of course it's too late now. But I wish you could at least know this about me. I tried. I did try.

Before it happened, I never knew anything about who Evelyn might really be. That was my half-truth to soften the shock. I told myself I hardly knew her. Just our group meetings, the few dinners. But she was one of us. So it was more than sad for us. Literally unbelievable. "Nothing is going to change," you were saying. Evelyn would still come to the group, still see patients. But we walked out stunned. Didn't you think we'd feel this? You must have. Evelyn was always right there, right along with you and right along with us. I'll say this, when things were normal, I know she enjoyed the work as much as any of us. And she was better at it than most of us, for what that's worth. Anyway, it hit us hard. I had a dream around the time things were happening between the two of you. I'm trying to sing "Stardust" to Evelyn but I can't get it started right. I keep having to start over. Then I notice that we're standing by a big lake and out in the water there's a tiny kitten swimming. Around its neck it has a fine ribbon that's attached a few feet back to a heavy office chair and it's trying to drag the chair through the water. I realize the kitten is going to get exhausted and drown so I run and jump into the water and start swimming out to rescue it. I never knew I felt that way about Evelyn.

♦

You know for a long time you were supposed to have the steadiness of the ocean tides. That was you. We looked to you for that. And Evelyn was a part of it. But what made you? I can't tell you how many times I've puzzled over that. What was your vital principle? And who was it wounded you? Must have happened. But then comes this. I don't think you predicted my reaction would be so powerful. I didn't either. A whole new chapter in my study of Romano. After you separated and after you moved, I imagined all kinds of things. It would dawn on you, you'd see what you'd done, you'd have terrible regrets. I knew nothing. I was caught up in things, cases and all the nonsense. But now, one word kept coming to mind, pity. The only way to name it, for both of you. And you do feel pity at something like this, like you're seeing a crippled animal, injured, trying to move. Because of the trouble you were in, both of you. Dani told me something later, after the bombshell. She said you were talking about what happened. She said you smiled helplessly. "I fell in love. It was at a conference in LA. I met someone and I fell in love. These things happen."

♦

I cared, for God's sake. Why does that sound so strange? My effort was too late, but at least I tried. I have to say, it was hard to hear all the sarcasm, or actually the venom. Venom is what it felt like. I guess I hit a nerve.

"Oh, so the therapist wanted to help, did he?"

"Yes, I suppose I did."

"You think I'm one of your sorry patients, Cyril?"

"Of course not."

"Do me a huge favor, okay? Perhaps you can just occupy yourself with your own business. That'd be a relief to everybody."

"No one is meddling in your life. I'm not. I'm not picking sides. I feel bad for the two of you."

"No need to."

"Well, feelings are feelings."

"Oh. Feelings are feelings. Brilliant." You went to the door. "I have to go.  And I really didn't need this little talk with Evelyn and myself. Neither did she."

"It's clear you didn't. But I might ask her what she thinks."

"Your business. I wouldn't bother."

Nice way for two colleagues to talk. I didn't know you, as much as I wanted it. I wondered if Evelyn really did.

◆

I thought things were getting strange that winter. Way off. There was that last dinner. What was that all about? Something had to be up. Obviously you both knew. But what was it? Maybe one last try for the two of you? Maybe if you act generous and normal it might be healing or something? The question is how were you both feeling? This was before you spoke to us. Because Dani and I didn't know anything. You guys were funny, by the way, inviting us not realizing the situation. You knew we became good friends later. Anyway, that night you could cut the tension with a chain saw. I remember a little thing. I asked Dani later but she didn't see it. So I probably imagined it. I thought I saw Evelyn's face practically drop onto the floor every time she left the table to get something from the kitchen. Completely wiped clean of any expression. And she was slowed. She was sleepwalking through it. I remember the meal and the whole scene, with your faded prints around the room. Epitaphs for something wounded and dying. It was all dead. The lifelessness of it all.

◆

It was a couple of weeks before that, Evelyn and I were having coffee in the diner. I was telling her about the Siegels. I don't have to tell you she was a good sounding board. I'd just gotten that couple. They were on the brink of separating. "Sounds rough," she said. She looked strained. "I have one like that. The 10-year-old burned his arm on the stove. A desperate little gesture to keep them together." Suddenly she had tears. I said, "Hey, you okay?" She shrugged and wiped her eyes with the heels of her hands. "Nothing. I'm sorry. It's nothing." Outside, she walked down Columbus saying she had some errands.

◆

She and I had quite a few coffees together later on. And we shared cases, but I never brought up the cries of pain I'd started listening for. We were talking on a different level. She had her own angle and her own kind of facility. This was the real Evelyn. We'd take out our coffees and talk in my office or her office. You knew about it. Probably from her. I'd talk about this case or that case and she'd hear me out and say things. And you know what I gave her? Appreciation. She got something out of it, sharing her own ways of handling things with me. She wasn't mentoring me but in a way she was. I never used a fraction of what she told me. I guess it all started when she told me I was warm. I actually asked her. She said, "Of course. You're a warm person." I took that to heart. It helped. So we'd talk and she'd point out better ways to put things. Polishing my words, giving me better words, more to the point, hitting the nail on the head. I never knew her to be so deep. I never knew she could be that blunt. She'd just say to a patient, 'How come?' or 'What just happened here?' or 'What were you feeling right then?' Or she'd say, 'What does that feel like?' or 'What is your understanding of that?' or 'We need to find out why' or 'Maybe we can think of something.' I loved it. She was fluent with it. I remember she once said, 'Any little feeling is better than none.' Something to remember when people didn't give out a lot of emotion. She said she always told patients you're more yourself when you feel your feelings. It was good to hear that kind of thing. I was in a muddle with one of mine and Evelyn said, 'Just try to find the person somewhere in all that.' If I was headed in a good direction, she might say, 'Yeah, go down that avenue.' She'd cheer me on. 'Stay with that,' 'Go after the feeling,' 'Deepen it,' 'Underline it.' She could correct me and it never bothered me. I once told a patient something like, 'So your mother is pretty bossy with you.' Evelyn said, "Too mild, Cyril. How about, 'It's clear your mother pissed you off, but you went ahead and put your foot down.'" And she'd catch me in my blunders. Never hard to find, like not paying attention, missing the point, wandering off to who knows where. Some of my trademarks.

♦

But the cries? You were the only one I wanted to share them with. I wish you had realized. I thought you would understand. They were shading everything, working on me. I was onto something crucial, something deep, absolutely astonishing, but it was disturbing. I wanted you to understand them with me. And even help me understand. I needed a comrade, Romano. And the thing was, I was finding that they weren't always there. I didn't always hear them, no matter how I listened. Why would that be? Even now I couldn't say. I never knew when it would happen. I just kept trying to do the work, case by case. But it was getting harder.

◆

I saw fifteen-year-old Eden around then, who stayed up all night and slept during the day. Again, she was one who didn't last very long. What was it, two months? Or maybe it was just forty-five seconds. Nothing substantial about Eden. There was something airy and filmy about it all. It seemed like she was walking in a dream. I got the feeling we were both in a dream. I saw her around five in the afternoon just after she woke up. She was a tall, very slim girl, gentle, quiet, with long blond hair. She was normal looking. She said she'd had her upside down schedule for about a year. She took it as reasonable. I had no idea. Neither did her parents. Did she have any friends? None that they ever met. She spent a lot of time on the computer. She was okay coming to see me, but she was dug in about her schedule and didn't see any problem. It was just the way she was. Don't keep bothering her about it. The school sent a teacher to work with her a couple of hours most afternoons so she could keep up with her class. I asked Eden if there was something that happened somewhere, something she had to avoid. But no, nothing. Did she feel safer at night or during the day? She feels okay. Not the slightest clue from her, nothing about anything. Any little change I suggested would be out of the question, like try waking up a half-hour earlier. No, why do that? So maybe it would all work out. She seemed like a decent kid. For a time she just had to live away from the daytime world, the world of parents or whoever. I suppose people find their way. Eden wasn't happy. I told myself for the time being she was doing her best. So sad and mysterious, Eden my dream ghost.

♦

Then you gave me little Niko, so bereft by loss. Niko, my little man of five who wouldn't talk, and we both thought he would be easy for me. He sort of was. Except he didn't want to talk. His mom was a nurse with long hours, a single mother. She couldn't get him to say a word. It started when the live-in babysitter left for South America. There was no notice, no warning, no preparation. So for Niko everything is snatched away. His world is torn in half. The ground opened up. With me, though, he acted fine. He even seemed happy, the little guy in his school trousers and little white shirt. But I couldn't get him to talk. I was down on the floor with him for weeks, playing with soldiers and spacemen. We set up little fortresses that had to be stormed and defended. It was fun for him. Sounds started coming out, grunts and growls, explosions, other noises. I thought he might be getting somewhere. He was making sounds that sounded like feelings, but so far no words. It didn't move fast enough so his mother took him to a psychiatrist and just a day or two on some tranquilizer and he's talking a blue streak. The dam breaks and everyone is relieved.

♦

And another one with a sudden loss. Jenny's thing wasn't as bizarre as little Niko's, but screwed up enough. Twelve-year-old Jenny. I like to imagine things got better for her, after she left off seeing me, but who knows? Maybe you heard the aftermath. I never did. This was all I knew, that Jenny's grandmother died very suddenly. A heart attack. The grandmother had been doing for Jenny since birth, babysitting, getting her off to school, helping with homework, cooking dinner, everything. The actual mother was a lawyer, working at a law firm. Another mother with long hours. She was a rising star. So right after the grandmother died the girl becomes anxious. Extremely anxious. She hates going to school and misses days. She begins clinging to dad, who takes over from grandma as full-time caregiver. At night Jenny needs all the doors and windows locked and then they had to be double-checked to make sure. And still she winds up begging to sleep in the parents' bed. Then one day she broke her leg playing soccer. It wasn't clear how it happened. The game got too rough. Was Jenny maybe a little reckless? No, she wasn't reckless. She was just trying to get to the ball. But maybe it was accidentally on purpose so she wouldn't have to leave home at all. She was desperate. She really enjoyed playing. And it kills you, because this wasn't a happy kid. The father wasn't happy either, being caregiver and working from home. Both parents were unambiguously pissed off when I said mom should try to spend more time with Jenny. That ended a session and they didn't come back.

◆

Remember Claudia Auster? She stays with me. Fetching charmer. Looking at her you'd never know she had a care in the world. She was cute and very funny, but flighty. I saw her starting to get impulsive. She had ideas about leaving school and working as a waitress. Or as anything. The parents were worried. She had no definite plan, of course. It changed from week to week, maybe day to day. Then there was a major crisis when her boyfriend told her he'd be going away to school in Albany. When he told her, Claudia tried to jump out a window. Then, for Christ's sake, she drank some Clorox. I don't know how much. Her mother had to stay home from her job and watch her. I spoke to Claudia on the phone and she laughed it off. All I could think was to have everybody come in for a big pow-wow. They wanted to do the right thing. So a week later they're in the office, mom, dad, little sister, boyfriend, and Claudia. They all settled in and arranged themselves. Claudia didn't say anything and seemed quite embarrassed. No one said anything and nothing seemed to be happening, so I said why doesn't each person talk to her and tell her what they feel about her. And Claudia should hear them and see if she feels like saying anything. Everyone took it seriously. They cared about her. The boyfriend seemed like a mature young man. I forget his name. He was tall and quite calm, but he looked like he was in over his head. Which I could relate to. He tried to reassure her that he'd be back home for different breaks in the fall and they'd definitely be together then. The whole hour Claudia said nothing, but she wept when her parents told her how much they loved her.

♦

There was a pathetic family. Were you aware of these folks? The Brocks. A mother and two kids. It wasn't for very long and nothing much happened. The kids were the reason for the sessions. They weren't getting along in school, and both were distracted, not doing any work. The mom was a very large, open woman. She seemed to be the naturally jolly type, but she was on edge. She was trying to get by with her work as a phlebotomist. I think she made house calls and drew blood for doctors and hospitals. Apart from the whole family mess, I wish I could have given this woman just a grain of self-esteem. How could I do that? I think of a book. I should have at least bought her a paperback mystery or maybe something medical. You kick yourself. Anyway, she was very anxious and worried and the kids were depressed. They were about ten, the girl, and seven, the boy. They had some of mom's jolliness but they were nervous and irritable. The girl was biting her fingernails and getting stomach-aches. But they weren't about to take anything too seriously. That was mom's job. You could laugh at these two. They were large kids, tousled, plump, looking like a picture on a cereal box. Just a couple of kids, wearing their jeans and plaid shirts. A few times Mom would leave them with me and make one of her house calls in the neighborhood. So the sessions were a kind of babysitting operation. Good enough. I took them that way. I guess babysitters can soothe kids. In one session, Elizabeth had something she wanted to tell me and she didn't want her brother hearing it. I don't remember what it was. So I asked Jerry to wait outside for two or three minutes. He folded his arms and wouldn't go. I asked and then I insisted, "Please wait outside for a couple of minutes." I said it again, twice more, looking right at him, and he looked right back at me. The boy wasn't moving and Elizabeth was just sitting there. Brother didn't surprise her. So I stood up, went over to him and grabbed him by his two arms and dragged him out of the room. He was heavy. I got him onto the couch right outside. He didn't make a sound.

◆

So, all those kids. It's a different world, Romano. You ignored it or maybe you took it for granted. We never talked much about it, but I thought it was a special place. We didn't belong there. So what did we think we were doing? You feel helpless because you're just the onlooker while a kid is stuck in one torment or another, almost always because of the adults around them. And they're afraid to cry out to anybody because so many times no one is listening. I guess one way or another they deal with it. At a cost. We don't even know how. It's actually heroic. And we should learn from it, all the courage we see. Think about it. And all our talk? It doesn't even register with them, nor should it. We don't know the game, we don't speak the language. They're lucky in their world. It's magic, really. We have no right to break the spell.

◆

Two young women came in on a snowy Friday night and had just that one session. I don't remember even mentioning this one to you. Tracey was at New Paltz and Barb had just graduated. The two of them were desperately in love, and wouldn't it be nice to think the session that night somehow mattered to them? I wish I knew. They were infatuated. They could scarcely think about anything except each other. That's how overwhelmed they were. And from what they said it all seemed intensified a hundred times because they were terrified they might lose each other. Because Tracey was sure her parents would yank her out of school if they found out. They couldn't pour out their story fast enough. A couple of times Barb said, "We're just trying to figure this thing out." They'd been trying to meet near the college. Barb could drive up to their rendezvous. They were full of strategies and sweet, fragile hopes for these meetings. So far they hadn't been able to manage it more than a few times. Tracey said she was panicked about flunking some classes, which would also be a disaster for them. Barb appeared the more sober and mature. She seemed steady and kind. She said that she and Tracey had talked it over and they were going to cool it a little so Tracey could focus on catching up with school. Barb seemed proud to be protective. We never got to anything more than this, not even how they'd met or how it had all happened for them. One session was it, because Tracey had to get back to school.

◆

It starts working on me. It must have been that spring, March or April, the whole suicide thing. Ideas bubbled up day after day. What did it mean? Was I letting people down? Look at my people. Ann, of course, but look at Debora. And there were others. Steven in the back of my mind. From your point of view, it's a big clinical theme. I started thinking you might have something to say about it and we could use your kind of tools, if you had any. I don't think suicide ever came up as such, which is ridiculous if you think about it. Why you didn't think to help us? It would have been a relief to know something to come up with when patients talked about it. The whole thing scared me. I always thought that would be the worst thing that could possibly happen to a therapist. Losing a life when you should have saved it. But of course the real tragedy is the person's death. And who knows about our own thoughts? It happens to us all the time. But day after day, I couldn't stop thinking about Steven. He'd talked about his fears from the beginning. His doubts, fears of suicide, not making it, fears of death itself. Fears about himself and about his sister. Total confusion about what his mother did. And him having no idea why. But how could he, at that age? And then didn't most suicides have a family precedent? Where did I read that? You hear about parents leaving a note blaming a child. At least Steven was spared that. Kids always blame themselves anyway. Imagine the wound when a kid is abandoned like that. It doesn't even have to be suicide. Mom gets an illness or something, anything. Kids will think they did it.  Imagine Steven at nine or ten. You know nothing, you're helpless. So, like I say, it started working on me. Nights in the office I started poring over the file. I was reading through all the notes. I was weighing Steven's words, going over them, trying to remember his mood, so flat to begin with, but trying to read between the lines. My imagination started running wild. What did I miss? Were there any clues? Of course I found things, as well as a lot of stuff that wasn't there. All his feelings, the real and the imagined together, but I'm in an unreal place. The good sessions, the bad. The good and bad together. I found a lot of my slip-ups, even fears of his that I had missed, different illnesses. But what was the plan if I did find something? What if I saw a wish underlying things he talked about, or a hint or a trend? What would I do? Go and try to find poor Steven? Draft him back into treatment? We did try to locate him afterwards. I asked Joan to contact him. Neither of us had any luck. And I'd gotten very shaky about him. What went into this state I was in? I fixed on one of the early sessions where I saw a comment, "I never showed emotions about my mother." There it is. So the shock didn't sink in. He never came to terms with it. His mind never processed it. The note read, "I just went along with it and never dealt with any of it." This was accurate. Exactly the Steven I knew. I never recalled him showing any emotion about it at all.

And this was his mother. Not the slightest tear choked back. Steven never even had that. He sat on everything. The trauma must still be buried. Sickening that I missed all that. But one night it hit me. I'm trying to digest it and I get agitated. I rushed outside and walked up the block and came back. I stopped in front, trying to get a grip. I looked up. There was no light in your office. It had started to rain. I thought I should go home. I went back in. It was after midnight and everyone had left. I went down to my office and sat on the couch. Was Steven at risk? Or was it possible he had moved beyond it? That would be wonderful if that happened. Is that possible in these cases? Was it likely he got more help? I know he never resolved it with me. Did he afterwards? Maybe he did, a little at a time. He might have handled it like that, a little at a time. I should go over the notes in the morning. I stretched out and fell asleep. I was drained and my clothes were wet. I woke up at dawn with my jacket over my head. It was a bad night and I wanted to talk with you about it. And then we couldn't find Steven. He was out there somewhere.

◆

There were so many I never should have taken on. Nobody should or could. You knew about some of these horrors. You might have warned us, but how would you know in advance? I told you later I had a rapist. Scary as hell. He told me he held a screwdriver to a woman's neck in an elevator. Imagine hearing this. Jesus. Put yourself in my place. I froze. I'm saying to myself, 'Just get me out of here!' He was tall and skinny with a narrow head. Snake-like is a good way to describe him. The thing is, why would he bother to come in and tell me this unless he saw some kind of problem? Or wanted help? He knew he couldn't stop himself. Not for me. He was gone, after one session.

♦

Then there was Peggy Williams and her morning depression. She said it had gone on for years. And she really suffered with it. You remember Peggy, the chef? Actually, she was a private cook for different families and she worried about keeping her jobs. "It still comes," she was saying. "It happened three weeks ago. I try to work around it. It's a dark pit I face in the morning. There's something about getting up that terrifies me. I have to leap over the pit just to get up in the morning. I call it a pit. I see it open up in front of me and it's deep. It's dark and deep. It makes the bottom drop out of my stomach."

I said, "That's awful."

She said, "I think this must happen to a lot of people, but if I don't make it, I'm just lost for the day. And if I miss the day's work I've lost the client. It takes everything I've got to make the leap. I guess it's a leap of faith that I'll have another day and things will be okay for me. I can't explain it. Why do I get a pit in front of me? I mean, where is it?" Peggy looked down at the floor and gave a wave of her hand as if the pit could appear right there in the room. She said, "It's bad. I feel like a pit is really there. I can see it. I could get swallowed up in it. There's no sense to it."

"Remind me. When did it start?"

"A long time ago. There were plenty of times I didn't make it. I wouldn't be able to get out of bed. Those days I have to stay in bed. Or I could get up but I might have to go right back to bed." And as if this weren't bad enough, Peggy had this other symptom, her hands sweated. She showed me.  She held out her small pink hand and sweat dripped off it. She said that didn't happen all the time, just when she was nervous. She looked over at me. I should say something. I wondered what it should be. She kept looking at me. I said we should keep talking about these things.

♦

One or two paranoid. That was plenty. You must have had some like this. They put me out of my depth. What can you do? That woman, what was her name? Wechsler. She'd go on and on till I was lost in the tangle. She'd sound desperate to make her point. "The jerk tried to destroy my reputation. Some people believed him. I don't know what he was saying but I guessed from the reactions of people. They weren't themselves with me. Outside, people have everything set up. It's weird. I go into a store, they give me the wrong change. And this security guard in the building where I work? There's something just not right about him. I mean he's so creepy. He looks like a killer or a psychopath or something. Just the way he looks at you and skulks around. To tell you the truth, I've started to feel like my back is against the wall. It's not that I'm evil. Maybe I do feel evil sometimes, but not really. People test me. They're acting strange. It's getting very annoying. They test me to see if I'm jealous. If I don't go near them, they'll think I don't like them. Or when I speak up, I'm the bad guy. Information is being fed by someone. Somehow they're getting information about my life. They know my business. They're acting like they have my thoughts in their brains." She'd go on like that. Wild. You could never sort it all out. Every single thought colored by her fears. She was trapped by them. It was hard to picture how she got through a day. If she saw something on TV about women getting attacked or imprisoned by psychopaths, she'd be sure it could happen to her. Her suspicions followed her everywhere, of course. She told me about staying in a motel on a business trip and there were people outside who kept brushing her window all night with a tree branch to annoy her and keep her awake.

Please. What do you do?

♦

And then that strange bird Norman. I don't remember him very well. I felt off-balance with him. You couldn't tell where he was coming from. He was a spacey young guy, early twenties, who talked bizarre stuff. Including once going AWOL from a psych ward. He wore good clothes that didn't quite fit. They looked as if they were bought for him by someone else. His family supported him. He didn't work. A session with Norman would wander from one thing to another more or less randomly.

"Why are you so nice to me?"

"You think I'm nice to you?"

"Yeah."

"Well, why shouldn't I be nice?"

"I don't know. I don't know if we have a therapeutic relationship. Do we have a therapeutic relationship?"

"Well, what do you see as a therapeutic relationship?"

"I don't know. I'm not sure."

"It's something we should think about, right?"

"Yeah, I suppose. But you know, what helped me was when I was in my program. It works. You train your neck muscles to stop you from stuttering. I did that."

"That's great, Norman."

"Yeah, it was. Now I'm starting dance lessons."

"Really? What made you decide to take dance lessons? Do you like dancing?"

"I'm not sure. I thought it's something I should know. It should help my social life."

"Okay."

"Yeah, it's down on Broadway in the fifties. I've only gone there once."

"I hope it goes well."

"Thanks." He stopped and looked at me. "I'm hoping this therapy will make a difference. Do you think it will?"

"Well, I mean, therapy, you know, is not of course magic. It seems to me you're doing quite a bit for yourself."

"I don't know. Am I doing it or is it just coming to me from the outside? I really don't know."

"Maybe a little of both?"

"Maybe. Also, I've been wondering if I should start law school. What do you think?"

"Law is a good career."

"Yeah, they make good money."

"Is that where the idea came from, the money?"

"Yeah, probably. Also I've thought about computer science."

"Okay. But, Norman, let me ask you. Have you ever had one of these tests where they test your vocational interests? It's that you seem like you're looking around for different fields. Maybe it would focus your thinking."

"Yeah, I've heard of that, too. I could do that. I asked my mother about the idea of computer science."

"What did she say about it?"

"All she said was, she said it's up to me, whatever I want. I was also thinking about Toastmasters."

"Oh? What is Toastmasters?"

"My program recommended it, like as a follow-up. It's a society for public speaking. I asked them, but, you know, I didn't, I didn't get a response yet. But I don't know if I need it, because I'm fluent enough."

"Yes, you are."

"So I'm back to square one. I've heard that law school is very hard."

"I guess it is, the pressure they put you through. And it's a commitment. Time and money."

"Yeah, I guess those are the deficits."

"But, Norman, I can see you're looking into self-improvement quite a bit, but you really also have a lot that's okay. I mean you're okay in and of yourself. You know what I mean?"

"I guess so."

And it went like that. We were talking but not hearing each other. He wandered with me for a month or two until he lost interest.

♦

I think of Cunningham, too. With all his talk, was he fooling himself? Or just me? He touched you even while you saw through him. All I could think was, Charlie was a fantasist, half quixote, half con man. I never had a clue what he was all about, let alone how to help. He was full of tall tales, like his stint in the Navy. Was he ever in the Navy? He said he was deployed somewhere and was told to kill a field full of pythons that reared up as tall as a man. That's hardly possible. Or when he was in a famous fire on an aircraft carrier. Or the story about a trip out west when he was learning to drive a big truck and he had to rush his supervisor to the hospital with a heart attack. He told his wife that was the reason he quit the job. Or being in a gang as a kid. I'm sure that was completely made up. For a while he seemed to like coming to see me. At least I was an audience. I started out believing him. You have to believe people. Until the tales piled up too high. But I went along. I thought bits of truth were coming out here and there. He started talking about marijuana, which he said he used a lot. He said he grew it under lights in a room in his apartment. Very doubtful. That had to be something he'd heard about. I actually did help him one day. Nothing to do with our sessions. This was a little job he'd gotten, to move a dining room set. I told you I was going to do this. We had to get it from Brooklyn to the East Side. Luckily it wasn't heavy. We got it all into the truck he'd rented and then brought it to the right building and took it up to the apartment. Driving a truck was a career Charlie thought he could do. So this was showing me his skill. He was nervous the whole time, especially driving the truck. He was chain-smoking. Not exactly talk therapy. At least it wasn't some tall tale. Then for one of his sessions he brought in his wife and stepson. He put on a show of asserting himself with the adolescent. The family played their parts. They loved the guy. Charlie lived in a cocoon that his family help him weave. I couldn't bring myself to break into it.

♦

Remember my orphan and grown-up foster child? That was Ryan, never truly connected with anything or anyone. He had lived his 40-some years isolated and lonely. He had foster brothers but they were out of sync with him. They didn't care. He lived with one of them after the father died, but that ended, and he would talk about how alone he felt. "I've been on my own since I was sixteen. No family behind me.  I had nothing. So I don't see how I'll ever get that stability, because I missed out on the family. I have no stable ground to stand on. I feel like I'm just barely keeping my nose above water." He was as vulnerable as anyone I ever knew. His worst fear was ending up alone. "I don't know if I'm capable of a relationship. Or capable of caring about someone. It's like I have a complete deficiency, to use that expression." One day he said, "I think Maury's dying was the tragedy of my life." About his foster father. Then he went back earlier. He started talking about the orphanage. A brutal and lonely place. "There was no one to talk to about anything. I don't know if you can really understand, but it was like such an abnormal situation there. Like the separation of the boys from the girls. It was like someone went to prison, but at least there you might have had some contact before. You might have gotten it with your family or at school, I mean walking to school or whatever. I feel like I missed out on everything that everyone else got." The children and the staff at the orphanage were mean. He described a long hallway he had to go through twice a day. It connected the dormitory with the school, and he dreaded going through it. The kids ran. He was slow and they'd have fun bashing him into the pipes that supported the ceiling every few yards. Ryan pointed to the permanent lump on his forehead from this. He wanted me to see the place so I could get some idea of what he'd gone through. It was a boarding school now. So one Sunday he drove us up there, about an hour away. It was in Rockland County. He'd gone there before. He had permission to visit, and he got us in. And he walked me through the hallway and showed me the pipes. He couldn't talk. His face was red and he was crying and his nose was running. This was a 42-year-old man revisiting childhood pain like we can't imagine. Acute pain. I thought the least I could do was try to understand what he'd been through. Remember when I told you about it? You had to tell me we didn't work that way. You said we help patients by talking with them and having them put their griefs into words. But what words does a 6- or 7-year-old have when his head is slammed into an iron pipe?

◆

What does that mean, getting overinvolved? You said I was letting myself get overinvolved. I hope so.  Yes, especially with Alicia. This kid spent a year crying. Sometimes uncontrollably, and from day one.  Sometimes ferociously. The situation she described would destroy anyone. You couldn't think of a worse horror movie. There was the incest and the baby that she'd had from it. She told me she would cry again and again to her mother, "Why didn't you do anything to stop it, you knew, you knew." And the horrific memories of the rapes. Her father would command her to move her body while he was raping her.

And the constant nightmares of the rapes, with her mother and sister just looking on and doing nothing. And then her longing for her baby, her three-year-old daughter with a disfigured ear. They told her she'd be able to keep the baby when she gave birth, but it was taken from her. She longed to hold it and comfort it. She begged and pleaded with her mother to tell her where the baby was. But she was never told. And the rage she felt. She said she wanted to kill herself after every single contact with her mother. "She was never there for me, and she beat me." But yet feeling she needed her mother. She begged her foster mother to let her have more visits. So she was torn in half by loyalty and hatred.  And she stopped trusting her mother at fourteen when the father's rapes began. It was impossible to get over. Her mother promised her she could get the baby if she agreed to go back to South America. But how could she trust that? And how could she believe the promises that her father wouldn't be around? And her sister knew where her baby was but wouldn't tell her. And then more memories, inconceivably brutal. Her father bringing her to a hotel room and making her help him while he aborted one of the sister's pregnancies. And always more nightmares. "My sister's baby is drowning and I can't save it and then I get pulled under myself." Or, "A man is chasing me up a hill and he wants to kill me." Or, "There's a flood of water taking away all the houses, and all the bad people die, but then they come back." So this was Alicia, and these were the horrors she'd lived with. What was there to do but weep inside and listen? So I did. I listened to everything, her past horrors, her impossible choices. Torn between wanting to stay with her foster mother in New York, where she felt safe, and wanting to return to South America with her mother and sister because she felt they'd be destroyed if she got adopted. And always weeping about hurting people, and weeping for herself. This was Alicia, and I saw the living nightmare of her life. The nightmare she was still living. You never forget something like that. And what do you do? There was so much you missed, Romano. Like Alicia's story. There was so much I wish you had known. I know it would have made a difference.

♦

Sometime before summer we heard about Micki and her institute. She told the group the week it happened. "I've been asked to leave Psychoanalytic." I felt terrible for her. She was grim and pale, her jaw muscles clenched. "After three years." The way she told us it sounded like there was a wrenching end to her training there. She looked broken and humiliated. I have no idea what happened but you probably knew. Did it involve one of the other candidates? Some dumb misunderstanding? It was a huge blow to her self-esteem. She prided herself on being one of the insiders. She'd gotten to be the brilliant acolyte to Emmanuel, the head of the place. She admired him and his theories. She read all his articles. One of the times I had lunch at her apartment she showed me something she'd written in high school. She pulled it out of a carton. It was an essay on "Why I want to be a psychologist." She wanted that from childhood. It meant everything to her. But at least she stayed with us, whatever happened. And a while later she told me how very kind you had been. She told me you spoke to her about her training and her expertise and the institute. And you put the whole breach in perspective for her. She said you really helped her.

◆

Then one of your memos about twice a week. You listed only one of mine, Michelle Kovacs. The question is, why didn't I think it through, why did I push her? I wasn't myself at that point. I couldn't think. Why did I push her? I should have realized she shouldn't be pushed. Too fragile. Michelle had her brave facade but it was just a facade. Fragile is what she was. In fact, that was part of her charm, I have to admit. But you and your idiotic twice a week thing. You seemed to think more is always better. When in doubt throw more sessions at a patient. You told us, ask them towards the end of a good session, say you feel they could really use an additional session each week. But here's the thing. When I pushed Michelle, she had a good instinct. She had the common sense to question two times a week. She went along but somewhere inside she knew it was bullshit. She said, "The second time each week seems harder. It's uncomfortable. I don't know if I'm avoiding something. I feel like with one session I've done enough. I feel like it's a waste of time, like it's just deadwood. It doesn't mean anything. I know you have to get through a lot of deadwood before you get to something useful." Mind you, she had already nailed down the main thing, her accommodating, trying to please everybody. She's the one who got to that. I'm not sure exactly when she did it. It must have been over a period of time. And here I was pushing her, asking her to accommodate to me. Not so great. Anyway, when I say we should try another session every week, of course who needs it? She questions, she boggles. She sees through it. She's about ready to say screw the whole arrangement. "Having to pay someone to listen to me, it seems like something's wrong with that. I feel like you wouldn't listen if you weren't being paid. You don't interrupt me, like my sister would, because you're being paid. Maybe you don't care. Actually I might even be more comfortable with you not caring, being just neutral. But the extra session makes me think you're a money-grubber. Also it makes me feel you're telling me I'm really sick. I don't like that. I think my problems are trivial, so either you're making too much of them or maybe it's much worse than I thought." But she goes along because she doesn't want to rock the boat. She said, "I still want to come once a week, but, okay, we'll continue at two times until further notice."

◆

I was in a bad place, Romano. Very bad. I felt like I was losing myself and I don't know what else. Gracia should have been my last. If I'd only known myself a little better. But how could you not do for her? She wasn't there to waste anybody's time, she was asking for help. I still see her round face and her reddened cheeks, the coarse black hair, plump shoulders, flowery blouses. So we start and I hear her talking about her father back in the Caribbean beating her viciously with a broomstick and she'd be trying to put her mind elsewhere. And then she's talking about her drug husband rolling in cash. She said, "I knew about it. I knew when we got married." But he became cold and distant and never talked to her and she lost all interest in him and never grieved when he got killed in a drug altercation. She got his money, or a lot of it, which made her all the more nervous. Gracia was a dignified person. Of course she was shy and frightened, but also strong and stalwart. She was strong in ways you and I aren't capable of understanding. We should have learned from people, Romano. Gracia faced whatever might come up. Even though it might be hard. She knew it was up to her to make herself known. And she trusted me. Sometimes she missed sessions but I didn't pry. She had her reasons. She talked about sewing clothes for a niece of hers who lived in her neighborhood. Who I found out didn't exist. Gracia told me later. She never laughed that I remember. Even though she always seemed cheerful. No, not exactly cheerful. Uncomplaining, not putting her troubles on anyone. We can't say as much.

♦

I couldn't lose Gracia. I was trying to hang on. It seemed to be going along. She was talking about issues, but she kept missing sessions. I don't think she wanted to, but she'd miss the odd session here and there. One week she missed and I called and she apologized. "I really don't know what happened. I thought it was another day. I don't know why." Three weeks later she missed again and when I called there was no answer. I called a few more times, still no answer. So I walked down to her building. It was the middle of summer and it was hot. She lived on Amsterdam in the high 70s. I buzzed her apartment. Nothing. I paced in front for a few minutes and buzzed again. Nothing. I shrugged and went back to the office. She came in the next Friday looking very tired. And she looked smaller for some reason. Like a smaller person.

"How are you, Gracia?"

"Not so good, Mr. Cyril."

"What's the matter?"

"I don't know."

"Did something happen?"

"I wasn't feeling too well."

"I'm sorry. You missed and I worried. I worried if something happened."

"I know. I'm sorry. I lose track."

"You forgot we had the appointment?"

"Yes. I'm sorry. I forgot the days. I'll tell you what happened. I'm embarrassed. I fell asleep in the bathtub."

"Really?"

"Yes, that's what happened. I woke up and I'm sitting in the bathtub. The water's all drained and I've had my period. It's all dried blood. I don't know how long I've been there."

She wasn't as shocked as I was. A couple of weeks later she didn't show again and I called. No answer so I walked to her building and was surprised when she buzzed me in. I walked up the stairs and knocked on her door and waited. She finally came to the door and opened it slowly. She was wearing a long robe, down to the floor, and she had a big kitchen knife in her hand. Christ. I thought for a second she was going to stab me. But she let me in and rushed back and sat down on the couch. She looked frozen in terror.

"Gracia, what's going on?"

She looked up at the ceiling and clutched the knife next to her. She glanced at me.

"Gracia, could you tell me what's going on?"

"They're here all day. Can you get them away?" She didn't look away from the ceiling.

"What's here?"

She nodded at the ceiling and the walls. "See?"

"I don't see anything."

"The animals. You see them? Get them away. Can you do it?"

"Gracia, I don't see anything. There's nothing there."

She said she saw snakes hanging down and rats and all kinds of lizards and spiders and scorpions crawling along the top of the walls around the room. She said they had been there since she woke up.  She said it wasn't the first time. She was afraid they were going to drop down on her and bite her and poison her. I tried to tell her there was nothing. She didn't believe me. I told her I'd keep guard in the living room while she got dressed. And we'd go to the hospital. I said these things were very common. The doctor would talk to her and tell us if she needed some medication. So, like I told you at the time, that's what happened. She was still terrified but she trusted me. We got a cab to the ER at St. Luke's. I said, "She's my patient and I'm her therapist," and the doctor examined her. He talked with her. He had her try to remember words he gave her and had her walk a straight line with her eyes closed and a couple of other things. Probably a standard test. At the end he prescribed a tranquilizer and she thanked him for it. She thanked me over and over. After that things ended with Gracia and me. I really miss her. One of the real ones. Gracia. In one of our last sessions, she took out a map and unfolded it on my desk. She asked me which property I wanted. It was a map of a lake in the Poconos with plots of land laid out all around it.

◆

Each was my last. What kind of tipping point. You had no idea. Or maybe you did. These things happened, Romano. I'm afraid it sounds like I made it up or dreamed a lot of it. Did Michelle really tell me that? It was when she was ending with me. She told me you said something when she was first starting. You could switch therapists for her, something to that effect. Like, let me know how it is in a month, I can change therapists for you if you want. Now why would she tell me something like this? I thought you didn't know her. Were you at her intake along with Carl? Did you say it to her later? Maybe Carl said it. Or did you tell him to say it? Who the hell knows? I never really understood. What bloody ground was I standing on? Were there any others you steered away from me? Michelle was one I liked. I miss her. First there was the twice a week thing. She was dubious and I saw it coming. She knew she didn't want it. She said, "After the first time, I don't have anything to say. And there's something about the closeness of two times a week. The closeness with you. I don't like being the focus. I don't care for it." She was going along but she was crystal clear. And then a few weeks later she decided she could do without our brand of snake oil altogether. She said, "I feel good. I know I have more to work on. But for now it feels like the right thing. I'm dried up right now. I don't feel like any more attention needs to be focused on me." Before she quit, I came up with something we tried for a few weeks. It was about trust. I started reading her my session notes. At each session I'd read her the last note and we'd talk about what went on. Why not level the playing field? Nobody's the boss. It didn't help. Twice a week had already done the damage. Plus, there was still the fee. She wanted copies of all the notes so I made copies for her. At the end she told me she'd gotten a lot out of our sessions. She was glad she'd stayed with me and didn't pay attention to what you said. It makes absolutely no difference now. But Michelle was someone I really enjoyed. I was hearing her and she knew I was. We were tuning in. After it ended, she sent me a card thanking me. I just don't know what really happened. Fumes of smoke. I had no idea what to make of it. And I was having hard times with all of my people. And myself. Desperate times. There's a tipping point and I was getting close to it. There's the point, true or not, when you need the patients to stay afloat. You depend on them. I kept telling myself, you can't be using their pain to help you get through your own. Not fair to them. You can't use patients that way. Has to be quite destructive.

◆

People don't realize. I heard David's cries. The day he's suddenly at my door. You never knew what went down. No one knew. But I did try. He's suddenly there, wobbling and wavering, probably an hour late. So I come out from behind my desk. "David?" Then I say his name again, like, are you okay? I took a step toward him. He wasn't okay. He's clutching the door frame and staring. In his eyes he looks trapped. He doesn't know what's holding him there. I took another step. David's chest, his poor concave chest, is heaving and he's sweating. Strands of hair are plastered to his forehead. He stares at me and he suddenly gives out this long rasping noise from his throat. I say, "David, you want us to talk? Let's talk." He started to move. He's bent forward and he starts shuffling. His sneakers are catching on the carpet. He's looking straight ahead and he's making his best effort to move forward. The smell hit me full on. He'd shitted himself. His blue running suit had dark stains all down the backs of the legs. He keeps on, aiming himself at one of the chairs near the desk. I pulled the chair out to give him a better shot. He made it to the chair and backed himself up and dropped down into it. He curled his legs under it and wrapped his arms around himself. He closed his eyes. Then he started rocking back and forth. I sat down in the other chair. I should have called upstairs. I didn't. And it's history now. But I wish you knew what the two of us went through. Anyway, now David starts shivering and shuddering. He's rocking back and forth and he's still holding himself with his arms. I'm just watching. Then he starts plucking with his fists at his shirt. He's grabbing handfuls and letting go. I had no idea what was happening. He tore at himself and got more and more frantic. Suddenly his throat rasped again. He throws his head back and comes out with a wail. People must have heard it. I pulled back. Then he twisted toward me. You knew he cut my face. His arm swung out and I felt the swipe across my face. He had a pen in his hand. I touched my face, my fingers were covered in blood. "Jesus Christ." I'm up now. I shouted at him, "What are you doing?" He dropped the pen and lunged at my hips with both arms. His head was down and he was gripping me for dear life, pushing me back onto the chairs. I didn't have much room but I managed to land one good right fist to the side of his head. And then another one, harder. Then one on his back. I wanted to hurt the son of a bitch. He went down and rolled over and lay on his side in front of the chairs. His eyes were clenched. It sounded like he was whimpering to himself. Then he pulled his knees up and lay still. Two steps and I'm out.

# I always wanted to have you out at the lake.

With Evelyn. We could have had some good talks. I always wanted that. It would have been nice. It's too late now. Species of can't forget. Can't and won't.  It's been too late this long, long while, hasn't it? Anyway, I was grateful for the time off. And for a chance to be alone. I needed that. I've thought about what might have been. I know you haven't. But if you ever had come out, just to spend some time, there's the dock to sit on and you'd feel the air, feel the peace, the quiet, watch the currents and the ripples and whatnot. You can let out your breath. Colors are always shifting out there on the water. You see bluish greys, greenish greys. I know you both would have liked it. In the morning a grey mist drifts over the surface of the water. For a little while you see only patches of water through the mist. From the end of the dock, you can see both ends of the lake, east and west.  Or put you in the boat just to drift all afternoon. You could drift through the drowsy, weedy lake for as long as you liked. Late afternoons are calm out on the water. You could go into the coves covered in lily pads. You could see our one little island out there with its few scraggly trees. It gets overrun with turtles, tiny ones, certain times of the year. Or row along the south shore past the stone house up on a rise. It sits there crumbling, with gaping windows and half-built broken walls. The aborted wreck of someone's folly. The stones are mostly green with lichen. Or you could pass through the narrow neck on the opposite side, into the lagoon full of weeds we used to call the little lake. There's a view to the west all the way down the lake. Evelyn could have taken some good pictures. You see the afternoon sun glinting on the water.

◆

I was in a stupor lying on the sunporch. Most days. Lost days. The only thing I thought was, this is where I am. I'd gaze out at the water through the dusty windows. I'd look over at the fir trees on the peninsula. I watched a bird one afternoon at the top of a tree over there. It was clutching a big fish against the branch, tearing at it, devouring it, tearing at it methodically one bite after another. It seemed to be taking forever. I stopped watching. The trees over there slowly lose their shape when the light fades. At night I'd hear the booming of the frogs, hollow booming sounds that had to be frogs. Also splashes in the water, calls in the distance, things you don't even notice after a while. When it rained I'd watch the branches of the maple just outside getting soaked and dark. Early one morning I looked across and saw two deer at the edge of the lake, one smaller than the other. They were half in the water, up over their front legs. They were plunging their heads under the water and coming up with the long, yellow stems of waterlilies. They would eat them and then get more, plunging under the water again and again. I watched a long time. I glanced away and they were gone.

♦

Days sweaty and agitated. Moods washed over me and went through me. They'd leave and come back.  The moods were murky. I can't say what they were about. Very veiled, muffled. They passed, but they'd be back. But to pull together enough calm so the moods and the solitude wouldn't be destructive. I could do that. At this point the solitude and me, we belonged to each other. You can't think of the past or the future. There wasn't much joy in the present, anyway, to feel deprived of. I wasn't sleeping. When I did sleep, a lot of nightmares. I can't remember. Vaguely one was hordes of crippled cats, hungry, with extra toes on every foot. Couldn't bother with that. But then the dream of my drowning when I was ten. I call it my drowning because it nearly was. Very nearly. I never told anyone. I hate the memory of it. And then it comes in my dream and I wake up sweating and remembering. I'm all alone swimming out by the dock one afternoon. There was no one to be seen anywhere. All was quiet. Just like when it really happened. I'm practicing holding my breath and swimming under water and seeing how far I can get without coming up for air. I'm doing that again and again. Then on one of these swims I come up underneath the lifeboat. I'm trying to push the bottom of it off the water to get a breath of air but I can't. It's flat on the water. The boat is a heavy, military lifeboat. This was my uncle's in real life and he kept it tied to the end of the dock. It had big yellow round inflated sides and a stiff rubber floor. It's like that in the dream. So I'd gotten myself trapped under the lifeboat. I'm trying to swim out from under the thing, but time and again I keep coming up under another part of the floor. I keep trying over and over. I'm desperate. I know I don't have any air left in my lungs. I make one last try. I get out from under and get some air. The dream was exactly like what happened that past afternoon.

♦

My mind was elsewhere. I burned my hand one night shoving a log back onto the fire. I kept forgetting to pull the boat up out of the water. One morning this huge dead turtle appeared, washed up next to the dock. It was more than a foot long. It was nauseating. A repellent monster, all bloated and shiny black and slimy, with a repulsive head protruding. I got it into a garbage bag and down to the trash. I can still shudder. At some point I started my walks. I got myself out in the afternoon. I had a route I began taking, heading west on the road that goes past the house, then passing the end of the lake and going up the long hill. The road up the hill was steep. Then I turned left onto a short road, badly paved with a lot of trees on both sides. This met another road that went back down the hill. So I got back to the house. It was almost dusk one afternoon coming back down the hill when suddenly I started sobbing. It was one of those spasms that blot out everything, everything you've been doing or thinking. It brought me to a stop. It was over quickly. I was still trembling when I got back to the house. That didn't happen again. At some point tokens of change started to appear. Of course you can't say how. What makes these things happen? Under the right circumstances moods must have a way of purging themselves. Or they reach a state of fulfillment and yield to something else. So there were these tokens of change. One day on one of my walks I saw something. A soothing sight. It was like a gift. Two horses, one brown and one white, were grazing in a clearing at the top of the hill. I saw them only that once. And then the leaves. I wouldn't have thought the leaves could smell so sweet. Tons of them underfoot. A peculiar medium to move through, the rustling and the aroma rising up to you in the cool air. Walking up the hill, hollow yourself out. Absorb it, feel your face and smell your clothes. This kind of thing could be calming. At least for me. So I can assure you changes did come about. Days huddling on the sunporch were not wasted.

◆

Megan called after I got back. She apologized. That didn't cut it and I told her. You knew they weren't very nice about it. You don't relish your work being called a farce or an abortion or worse. Criminal, demented. They seemed to take it personally.

People act in shitty ways, hurtful ways, but you have to let it
pass. Let it go by. You said that yourself. I forgave them.
Including Evelyn. No real animus left over on my part, as far as I
know. You've got to have your armor when you need it. And it
wasn't the catastrophe people said it was. Anyway, I know what
I know. And I really have started to let it go. The feelings come
near and rise in swells like waves, but we swim the tide. We
cherish our wounds and keep them close. And every sin carries
its own punishment, blah, blah, blah.

♦

I didn't know I'd be grateful being back, but I was. At least for
that first short while. And Tillie came in. That amazing and
problematic woman. But like I told you, I wasn't up for much at
that point. So why start me back with her? The harrowing
sessions she suffered through, harrowing for both of us. You
can't imagine them. I have to tell you it was confused and it
confuses me to this day. You'd think I'd remember how she
began. I've tried but when I look back I can't. And it's no
wonder. There were too many loaded sessions. One more
troubling than the last. I could never reconstruct how it went.
How would I? You wouldn't be able to follow the details
anyway. I couldn't follow them myself and I was in it with her,
right there, week by week, until the end. I'm guessing you would
have cared, but she was another one you missed out on. So
vulnerable and emotional, all her weaknesses showing. And our

sessions? It was like she wanted to throw her whole life at me helter-skelter. At times it was pure madness. By the time she came to me her whole life was whirling around her, whirling around in her head, and she was going to make her way through it come hell or high water. One day she said to me, "Therapy is for truth-telling." And I had to give her credit. She had a drive. She didn't know where it was taking her at any given moment and I certainly didn't. The things that happened to her. Her collection of people. The feelings she lived with. Or lived through or tried to live through. There was always so much confusion about what she was feeling. It was a mass of confusion. Chaotic feelings were what held her up, supported her and kept her going, but that makes no sense. There was something she said in our early weeks. She said, "My feelings are keeping me from my life. I know they're not helping me. I have to tell you, basically I haven't done what I wanted to do with my life, but don't ask me what that is."

◆

Yes, she was sad and depressed. You think that stopped her from messing with me? All the trash she could throw out. Misleading me, turning the tables, testing me, especially at the beginning. And there was always something behind it. I can only call it a bitterness. What could I do with that? Her moods could sail up and she'd rag me. I wasn't up to it. I never had someone like this before. I might say something like, "I think you're mocking the therapy today," and she would come right back.

"No. How would I manage that?"

"The jokes."

"What jokes?"

"Like calling your father the elephant in the room."

"Oh that. He was the joke. In my opinion. Really funny."

"Tell me about him. Was he always funny?"

She pouts. "Are you ever funny?"

"I don't know. When I'm in the mood."

"Be funny, then. Go ahead."

"Sure. No. I don't think so. We're actually here to work."

"Strange kind of work, I'd say."

She could dodge around like that. I wondered what was going on. I thought it was coming from moods of despair and bitterness.

"What do you think drew you to Rich?" I might try to explore her marriage like this.

"That's precisely what I want to find out."

"Well, let's think about it."

 "No, I know why I married Rich. I wanted to get married and he was around. I'm sorry I messed it up."

"I'm sorry. Did you learn anything from it?"

"I think so. You ever mess anything up?"

"Of course, like everyone."

"So now you know how I feel."

But she hadn't married Rich lightly. Far from it. Which I'd learn later, once she thought I was ready.  And she certainly never thought her father was a joke.

♦

Layers and hidden recesses, Romano. Who knows what all was there? There had to be a story in there somewhere but she didn't want to tell it. Or she wasn't ready. Or she wasn't up to telling it. That's not strange. Who's up to telling their story or even knowing what it is? Do people ever give us their whole story? I guess that's our job. And with Tillie, I've thought that would have helped her later. If we had been able to piece together all her sad piles of miscellaneous junk. But it's a question. Then always blaming herself, tons of blaming. All that talk in the group about the self-blaming that goes on. A vicious habit they called it. Is it a habit? Whatever it is, that was Tillie. At first I thought it would wear thin, but it never did. I think you knew about that. We sounded the depths, or we tried to. I'll say some of the depths, before the very end. You realize those are hard to think about. Tillie would stand back and then try to wade in as best she could. She'd tell me things like, "I have a lot of insecurity. My moods. There are days my body feels very tense and draggy. I'm not happy all the time. I get depressed. I feel helpless, like I've lost faith in myself. I get the feeling I was thrown off the horse but I'm afraid to get back on."

◆

One week Tillie starts talking about a middle school teacher, her favorite teacher, Mr. Carruth, who taught social studies. This came later on when she trusted me more. "He was so manly and cute," she said. "He wasn't that tall, but he had nice dark hair and big brown eyes." She had a crush on him. "We all did," she said. "He was boyish. We called him Andy among ourselves. He was our homeroom teacher. He had heavy eyelids and long lashes. He had a habit of pulling on his eyelashes, to pull out loose lashes that seemed to bother him. Whatever it was he was teaching, you couldn't help learning it. You didn't want to miss a class. I've forgotten all of it. It was about government and history. We paid attention. He had us do things. Like we wrote to a book company and asked where one of the photos in our history book came from." Tillie looked at me. Was I following? Then she said, "What was I like through all those grades? I was a tease and a flirt. That's just how I was. I knew what I was doing. Not with Andy. Oh God no, I hope not, not with him. But I'd show off my shape and toss my hair a lot. I'd pass notes to boys, like to Eddie. Eddie was handsome, and pretty serious, and maybe I wanted to stir him up. In fact, that's exactly what I wanted to do, at least get his attention. I was interested in him. I gave him a pamphlet that came with some Tampax I got. Showing female anatomy. One time I sent him a note, '*Te amo*,' I love you in Latin. So this thing happened. Eddie and I were staying late in Mr. Carruth's room. It must have been four-thirty or five. We were making posters for a bake sale. We were at the table in the back of the room. The one I was doing wasn't too great but that didn't matter, it was good enough. The class was trying to raise money for our trip to Albany. So we were drawing these posters on white cardboard. Eddie's was going to show the capitol building with huge cupcakes in front of it. Mine showed a bus on a road with kids waving out the windows. A sign on the side of the bus says To Albany. Then Andy came back and looked at what we were doing. I don't know if he was standing next to me or behind me. But he was awfully close. He was too close. He said, 'That's good, Tillie.' I'm sure his body or his stomach or something was right up against me. I felt him right against me. I was scared. I can't think about it. I kind of squirmed away sideways. I said I'd finish the poster tomorrow or something. I didn't tell Dinky. Actually I wasn't calling him Dinky yet. But my father, I didn't tell him. I didn't say anything. Not something like that. I tried to bury it. I had him call the school and get my homework for the rest of the week."

♦

Tillie kept trying to open up, patch it together, sort it out. "I always had to have a boyfriend," she said. "I needed instant gratification, emotionally and physically. So I'd pressure my boyfriends to see me constantly. I stuck with this one boy, Teddy, a long time, at least a year, or more than a year. I was fifteen when I began seeing Teddy and we were lovers. A very good looking boy, with curly hair. Both his parents worked so we hung out at his apartment. He was a video game addict. We drank too. I was very young but I drank with Teddy. Sometimes I was a little drunk at school. I remember one time my friend Faye smelled it on me. She said, "Have you been drinking?" I forget what I said. She was shocked. I was ashamed. Once we were drinking all afternoon, which we did a lot, but then we went to something at school. I fell down and went sprawling on the front steps. So embarrassing, right in front of everybody."

◆

At times she sounded reflective. Like when she said, "It's the same problem I've had all through my life, the way I deal with relationships. I mean with everybody, not just members of the opposite sex. I ruin relationships. I'll cling to a relationship too much. I'll ask for too much. I get very emotional. I lose my self-respect."

"Why do you think you do that?" I said.

"How would I know? I know I smothered Teddy too much. I thought we were close. But at the end he was the one who got tired of it. I clung too much. I started calling him when he asked me not to. I used to go over to his apartment uninvited. I don't know how many times I did that. I have to tell you about the low point. It happened one afternoon. It was so stupid. I called him and he didn't answer and I kept calling and calling and then I went over there. It was only about four and we'd always be together. So I went over there and I'm outside and I called. He answered and said he was busy with something he was doing. I said, couldn't I just come up and wait for him and then we could hang out or whatever. He said no, he didn't want that. I asked him please, but he said no. I promised I wouldn't bother him, but it was still no. So I lost it. I said, 'You're lying. I know you've got somebody up there and I want to come up and see.' He said he wasn't with anybody and it's none of my business anyway. I said, 'So I'm right, I'm right.' He hung up. Then I kept buzzing the intercom. No answer. Then I followed a woman inside and went up to his apartment and rang the bell and knocked. Again and again. He finally came and yelled through the door, he's not going to let me in and please go away. I said I just wanted to talk. I said, please, let's just talk. He yelled go away, go away. After a while I sat down and waited. It was a long time I just sat there. I found a flyer in the hallway and wrote a note and shoved it under the door. I wrote only one word, Goodbye."

♦

School loomed large and adolescence. There was a boy she knew in high school. He was important somehow. She was saying, "He was so sweet. He was very shy. We were riding around one night in Laura's car, her little Fiat, some of the group. Jimmy's in the front. I'm in the back with Annie and Ramon, and Annie starts chanting, 'Tillie's got red panties, Tillie's got red panties.' I had gotten my period. Everybody's giggling, including me. I'm sure Jimmy had no idea what was going on." She was talking about another time when there was a party at a friend's apartment. "We were all drinking, people are in the kitchen and the hall, and Jimmy Doshier and I are sitting just looking at each other in the living room. The music is loud. I don't think Jimmy was much of a drinker. We were making small talk about school and people. It was awkward. Do you know Kristin, do you like her, do you know Kenny, etc. Jimmy wasn't really what you'd call cute. He had a long face. He was kind of average. I was just there, nothing was going on. And him being so innocent, he just sat there like a boy scout until I left with some other kids. Nothing happened but I think he wanted something to happen. In fact, I know he did. But how was it going to happen? Nobody threw out any signals." Tillie stopped and I guessed her tears were coming. "Should I have done something? I couldn't. He had this awful crush on me, he was sick with it. I had an idea, but what could I do? I just didn't have any big feeling. Sometimes you just don't feel anything." And she wept over Jimmy. Jimmy, the innocent boy, and how he'd suffered because of her.

♦

And more about school. "I was too young. You're under pressure and I wasn't ready and nobody told me anything. I was alienated from the mainstream. I wasn't an outsider, but I felt like one. I remember the time my friends started saying I was loose and had developed a reputation. Some friends, right? It wasn't true. And then I lost all my friends when I invited this boy to a party who was outside our group.  They made an issue of it and ostracized me. I had met this boy, Jake, who was at Stuyvesant. It was no big deal, he shouldn't have been a threat. Jake was quiet. I think the girls were jealous. He was actually really well built. He had bad acne, but so what? I saw him a few times and we went to hear a singer he liked at a club. I told him how my friends were acting. He thought they were jerks and I agreed. He said, 'It's their undeveloped brains.' Anyway, for a while the main ones in our group stopped having me over, and I wasn't invited to any of the parties. I felt miserable being treated like that. Kids can be so cruel. It lasted almost to the end of the year. I was so relieved when it ended and I saw them again."

◆

She talked about someone else she went out with. "Ron seemed mature. He really seemed like a fine person. He was two years ahead of me in school. We had a good time together. I might have liked him as a boyfriend. But he started pressuring me to sleep with him. I liked him, but I didn't feel like being intimate with him, at least not so soon. He kept pressuring me. He just wouldn't let up. Then he became insulting. He actually called me a slut. I felt very dirty, really cheapened. It was very humiliating at the time." She would muse about why women allow themselves to be pushed around and dominated. She really wanted to explore that. "Why do we always have to be one down in relationships? We let it happen or else it just happens. They must have research on that. It makes no sense at all. Why do we let ourselves be smashed down?" She was disgusted and puzzled by it. But she said at one point she came up with her own answer. "The only answer is to act for yourself and not stay wondering. Be yourself.  So I had to pull into myself. I guess I started trusting myself more. Maybe I did. But that's it. You can't trust people. I trust Dinky, that's about it."

♦

"Dinky had girlfriends," she was telling me one day. "I even liked a couple of them. Carol the attorney was one. She was great. They weren't together that long. She gave me one of her white polo shirts and once she took me to the movies. She was like my older sister. I was thirteen. That was one girlfriend I wish had lasted. There was nothing wrong with the way she looked. I don't know why he stopped seeing her. I suppose you never know. Then there was the bitch who moved in. Direct opposite. The Margot person. Ugly bitchface. Where did he find her? I hated her guts. God damn her in hell. She thought she had the right to talk to me about what I did or didn't do. Who the hell was she? She was so full of shit. She was always trying to boss me. She'd say things like, 'You know your father's life is hard, being alone. You could do more to help.' She could start in on me. She told me one too many times, 'You never cooperate with your father,' and I blew up. I yelled right in her face, 'Mind your own goddamn business!' She just looked at me. She didn't talk to me for two days after that, which made me quite happy. Then there was a big blow up we had about vacuuming the living room. She says to me, 'Tillie, we have to discuss this.' I said, 'We have nothing to talk about.' She said, 'Your father wants you to keep the living room clean.' I said, 'He can talk to me if he wants to.' And she said, 'He asked me to talk to you about it.' I said, 'That's a lie.' She said, 'You don't talk to me that way.' I said, 'I just did.' And she raised her hand like to slap me. Stupid bitch. She thought she had a lot of power. And I know she told Dinky not to give me money. I told him how much I despised her and I think he started to see how she was. One night they were out and I went into Dinky's bedroom. The closet door was open and on the floor there were pictures of my mother torn to bits." Tillie was clenching her two fists so her knuckles got white. Her face was wet with tears. I couldn't say a word.

♦

The next week she wanted to talk about her mother. "Dinky would never say very much. I'm sure it made him too sad. When she died I was only five and a half. I try to remember her. And I do remember her. I can remember things. I daydream about her. I do that when I'm alone."

"What kind of daydreams?"

"What kind of daydreams? Like I'll look up at the sky and wonder if she's up there, or where she is. I'll think about her

holding me, maybe singing to me. Dinky said she was graceful, like a dancer, and petite. She had hair my color. Dinky says I have her eyes. He looks at my eyes and he sees her. She was quiet but people noticed her. Just because of the way she was. He said my mom had the most loving heart. He said, 'She always held out a hand to help people forget their difficulties.'"
"She sounds like a very loving person."
Tillie laughed. "I have memories. She taught me my right hand from my left, and how to put your shirt on so it isn't backwards. My mom loved me."
I asked Tillie her mother's name. I almost didn't hear it.
"Emma."

♦

One day she said, "Did you know I had a sister?"
"No," I said. "You did? For real?"
"Of course I did," Tillie laughed. "Well, no. But there was a girl. She would have been so nice to have as a sister. Patty, the sister of my friend Bonnie. I only met her once in my life. In the fifth grade Bonnie brought her to school one day. She never got to go to school. She was retarded. She was two or three years older than Bonnie. She was pretty. But she had to wear thick glasses. The teacher had Patty sit next to me the whole day."
"Oh?"
"Yes. I guess Miss Johnson thought she'd be okay next to me."
"And how was it?"

"It was easy. She was no trouble at all. Patty paid no attention to what the class was doing. She could talk but she was very shy. She just drew all day. She was very quiet. She sat and worked on a drawing of a horse's head the whole day."

"Interesting."

"Yeah, it was a beautiful horse. She worked on it. She kept her face close to the paper. She must have done this a lot at home. This was her skill. Just with a pencil and paper she brought out this beautiful picture of a horse. Its head and neck. I watched. She shaded it. It had that lock of hair between the ears. She did the nostrils, the big eyes, the mane, long eyelashes."

"It must have really been something."

"It was. It looked just like a real horse. It got better and better. Patty definitely knew what a horse looked like."

"Nice," I said.

"And you know what? At the end of the day, she said do you want it? She gave me the picture. I hugged her and we laughed and hugged. I was so happy. I couldn't believe it. I still have the picture somewhere. I'll show you if I can find it. Bonnie said we should all three of us get together. She'd ask her mother."

"Did you?"

"No. It didn't happen. Bonnie told me Patty was sent away. That was a sad thing. She was sent away to live with a family upstate. It was a family that takes care of kids like her. Up somewhere near the Adirondacks."

♦

Tillie talked about a dream journal she used to keep. She said, "Every morning I'd grab the notebook by my bed and try to write out any dream I could remember. It worked for a while. It was weird the way it worked. I remembered at least one dream every morning. Nightmares and others. A lot of bad dreams. In some of them I'm calling and calling to Dinky. Dinky help me, help me, but he can't hear me, he isn't there. I'm so scared. In one dream he is there and I'm climbing into bed with him so he'll comfort me. He tries to help but he's kind of half-hearted and I'm still scared. I remember he holds me, but his arms and his wrists are very thin and skinny, very weak."

I said, "You must have felt very lonely."

"I guess. There was another dream where Dinky is holding me to comfort me but another Dinky is there in the room. He's walking slowly toward us waving his arms up and down. He's very tall. He's some kind of wizard. He's holding long sticks in his hands, waving them up and down. He's dressed in white, in a long robe or something. It was eerie. There were so many dreams. Then I gave it up. The dreams were just going to go on and on, more or less the same no matter what. But I did jot them down for a while. So what the hell. There were some strange ones. I used to write poems, too, expressing my feelings."

I said, "Oh, really?"

"Sure. Here's one:

'You are not here,

You are not here,

Not here.

I don't know who is here,

Is here,

Is here.'

It's supposed to have an echo effect. And my visions of nature. I wrote about the flights of birds and other things. Here's one on birds. I'm up there flying with them.

 'With you wherever,

I give you myself.'

And it goes on. Things like that."

"Nice," I said.

"I showed Dinky and he really liked them."

"I'd love to see anything you wrote."

"I tore them all up."

"Why did you do that?"

"They weren't good."

"I would have liked to see them."

"Too bad. Anyway, they weren't for your diagnosis."

♦

I thought I started sensing more of the real Tillie. Her cries. Not just the stories she poured out. Her deepest joys and troubles, from her heart, spoken or whispered there among all the words she was saying. Like sighs between the words. You imagine things. But it seemed so real. Those soft murmuring sounds. That undertone. Something I was almost sure about. But you're working with someone and you do imagine things. Which even helps. It helps you to know the person. You would never admit that, being who you are. It doesn't even matter whether it's real or not. Think about that. What does it matter? It's all part of the process. So then what was it, a delusion, this undertone? Or a wish? If you could explain that to me. Of course, I know this had been a problem for me before. What's true between people? We might know each other much more than we think. Call it intuition or a vibe or anything you want. And why couldn't I be sensing these deeper things with Tillie, just like I did before? Her hidden feelings echoing between the words, the cries between the words. The words could be nothing. I remember asking myself, was there something more real there? There was no way to know. The things I used to babble about. Everything you used to say I made up. But what did that make me?

♦

One week she was talking about a summer romance. There was a boyfriend the summer before college. It didn't last long. Tillie said, "Justin was a nice guy. Tall and gentle. He was a gentleman actually. He was already at NYU and he was sure I'd love it there. I met him at a party. He was easy to talk to. I admit I had strong feelings. We started getting together at the apartment he was sharing in the village.  He had a job in some NYU office and I'd meet him after work, and then on weekends we started taking the train up to Mt. Kisco. To his parents' house. He grew up there. I liked staying in the house there. Both his parents seemed to like me. His mother was quiet but his father made up for it. Mr. Cameron was a blowhard, but still nice. He was a big man. He really liked to drink. After dinner he'd start drinking scotch. His glass was like a goldfish bowl. Justin's mom with her little drink would just sit quietly by and give him refills when he asked. He liked Justin and me to have a beer with him so we did that."

"Were they alcoholics?"

"You could say that. But what's an alcoholic? Mr. Cameron was a drinker, for sure. Anyway when Justin's job ended we thought we'd go up to the house for a week. The first Saturday Justin took me out to dinner in Mt. Kisco. His father let him have his big car, so it was an occasion. It was great. We ate in a Middle Eastern place. Then we went to this hang-out where we saw a lot of his friends. I met the crowd. I felt like I was fitting right in. Of course they had lots of in-jokes. They had funny names like Cricket and Zinky, and other things like that. Justin and I were keeping up with the drinking. But only beer. It was fun. I was feeling good. We left while most of them were still going strong. We thought we'd wind up the evening just together. I'll tell you what happened. Justin wanted to show me some of the areas with big estates around there. So we drove out into the country on the winding roads. I liked to snuggle up close to Justin. He was pointing out big mansions to me but you couldn't see anything but trees. After a while he said we'd better be heading back. We were on a small road and I thought he was going much too fast. I didn't say anything and he was completely quiet. I was still right close to him and I started playing with the radio. It was one of those where you push a button and it finds the nearest station. I was trying to get some good music and I'm playing with it and then WHUMP! BANG! We jolt straight up to the roof and rock back and forth against each other and then we pitch backwards. It was just a split second. And Justin is yelling get out, get out, and he's pulling me out his door. Sparks are coming down. And the car is stopped in the grass and we're running away from it in a field full of weeds. I started to cry. Something had happened but I had no idea what. We stop and look back. I'm hugging onto Justin and he's holding me. He's shaking."

I said, "My God, Tillie. Were you all right?"

She said, "We could have been killed. We almost were. It was terrible. Terrible, terrible. The car had turned around and jumped off the road. It backed itself into a telephone pole. We saw the back of the car split by the pole, all the way back to the rear window. We were afraid the sparks would make it blow up."

I said, "God! What a horrible thing."

"It was really bad. We were so scared. We kept moving back away from the car. The sparks stopped coming down, but we still didn't go near the car. We finally ran to it and I grabbed my bag and Justin got his phone and called his mother."

"You were so lucky."

"I know. I know. No one spoke going back to the house. I was in the back seat crying. I was awake till morning and still scared, thinking how we almost got killed and how I'm practically in Justin's lap and playing with the radio. So I guess it was my fault. I got a taxi to the train in the morning."

I said, "You were both very lucky."

Tillie said, "After that, we were over, Justin and me." She grew silent and she had tears in her eyes. Minutes went by. She finally said, "It's a destroyer."

"What is?"

"Love."

◆

"I was always desperate for at least one good friend," she told me. "A lot of the time I'd be friends with the kid that no one else wanted to be friends with." Now she was talking about a friend she had at NYU. They met the first week of school. Tillie had a lot of feelings for her right away. "We were simpatico," she said. "I latched onto her and she did to me. I was afraid, starting school. We both were." The friend was disabled. She wore specially built shoes, and Tillie felt sorry for her. And more and more sorry as things went along. She said, "I worried about Kaela's difference. I guess she didn't want to look concerned. But she must have been. Or she'd gotten used to it. Anyway these things don't matter. She could be very funny. She had a classical face. It was beautiful. I found out she was a genius in math, higher math, very advanced. You want to hear something really bad? I was embarrassed walking with her because of her limp. I tried to make it look like I didn't notice. I feel so ashamed." Tillie told me they stayed friends through school, but she said, "We never got really close. That was sad. We should have. We never did."

◆

It was too much to take in, Romano. What do you do with it? I was bombarded. She said, "It hit me the second week of class." Now it was the young professor, the professor she was in love with. She said, "This teacher fascinated me. I got obsessed. His name was Jonathan Landon, Dr. Landon. Physical Science. I couldn't take my eyes off him the whole semester. He was always late for class. Sometimes very late. He'd come in carrying his container of coffee and his backpack. The coffee dripped all over the backpack, which he didn't seem to notice. He'd scrawl the equations and all kinds of charts and arrows on the board, talking over his shoulder at us. He explained the way light bends in lenses and all that. Or else gravity and relativity, which I actually found fascinating. He didn't joke. He was a young teacher and he took it all very seriously. He was always in corduroys and sweaters. Kaela sat next to me and jabbed me with her elbow to stop me staring. I must have looked hypnotized. One week Landon was fifteen minutes late. The whole class decided to clear out and teach him a lesson. Even Kaela. They all left but me. I waited so he'd notice me. I was the only student in the room when he finally came rushing in. He was embarrassed and said something like 'Oh boy, sorry, I'll see you next time.' I thought I was making an impression, but that's null and void, when I look back. Or this was good. The time I went to his office supposedly to talk about the paper we had to write. I was wearing tight jeans and I had my old felt hat perched on my head. He was in his desk chair and I got myself standing in front of him, between him and the desk. Then I boosted my butt onto his desk and I'm sitting in front of him swinging my legs back and forth like I'm onstage. I don't remember a thing he said or I said. In my final exam book I wrote a love note at the end. Real kid stuff. That's all it was. I tried to make it sound sophisticated but very passionate. I wound up with a C."

◆

And then there was something she couldn't let go of and she'd choke up over it, this incident with Kaela. This was still sometime in the fall. Tillie thought she should help Kaela get her social life going and she got the idea of fixing her up with a student from her English class. This was a kid named Terry, a first-year like they were. She said he was shy and she thought Kaela and Terry might hit it off. Tillie said, "Kaela was very doubtful. I knew she was afraid. But I told her even if it came to nothing, so what." So she kept touting Terry, saying what an extremely nice guy he was. Finally, she coaxed Kaela to cook dinner in her dorm suite and she'd bring Terry along to meet her. The night of the dinner things seemed to be going okay. Tillie figured after they all had some ice cream, she'd just leave

Kaela and Terry together. She told them she had to get going. She said, "Why don't you guys finish up the wine?" But Terry had other ideas. He said he'd better get going, too. And the ending wasn't good. Tillie said, "There was this disgusting clown show when we're leaving. We have our coats on and we're heading for the front door, but Terry grabs a closet door by mistake and yanks it open. Oops, he laughs, and it's so obvious he had to get out. He had no interest in Kaela." The screw-up was excruciating. Tillie said she could never forgive herself. She couldn't let it go. What was it, survivor guilt, or some other kind of guilt? Maybe you'd have a fancy name for it. She said, "I was lucky to know Kaela and, what do I do, I turn around and hurt her. Right in her weakest spot."

◆

You used to tell us we're not here to judge. We always told patients, don't judge, don't judge. I judged all the time. I couldn't help it. People are always being judge and jury on themselves. It's what people do. Big surprise. We should just accept it and deal with it. Tillie wouldn't stop. I couldn't stop her. It made her feel better.

"I guess you see by now how worthless I am."

"How is that?"

"I'm a worthless person."

"Is that what you want me to think?"

"No, I just am. Don't you see that?"

"No. I don't see it."

"You say that, but you don't really believe it."

"Why is that?"

"Haven't you been listening? I've hurt people."

"You have?"

"Yes, I have."

"I don't think I'm as clear on this as you are, Tillie. Maybe you're wrong."

"Please, you don't have to play dumb. At least I know what I've done. I was there. I'm not stupid."

"You know, you might have a point there."

"Well, thank you. So, tell me, what would make me not worthless? After all the things I did. What? I'm asking."

"What do you think?"

"I asked you first."

"Okay. Maybe you are worthless, but you don't have to feel that way all the time. That seems unnecessary."

"Why? How am I supposed to feel? It jumps right out at you just looking at my life. Everyone I abused and mistreated. Starting with Rich. No, there were a lot before Rich. Like Kaela. And then all the money I borrowed and never paid back. From Dinky, and other people. How I treated people. People I used. One way or another. It's something to think about."

I said, "So what do you think about it?"

She said, "Also I'll get nasty and say things." She stopped. A different mood suddenly. She said, "I'm, you know, basically very shy. I really am. I can go from one extreme to the other with people. Basically I'm afraid of people."

I said, "Okay. You know what I think? I think you've got a lot of good you want to do for people. I think you've got good feelings inside. You know the expression, being hard on yourself? Let's hear some kindness towards Tillie."

She stopped and she seemed to take this in, but who knows? In one of these sessions she surprised herself and blurted out, "You're a nice man." But the next week she'd probably start in on herself again.

♦

Wouldn't it have been better for everyone if only she had quit? No great loss for her if she had. It would save her digging up so much grief. Some days I thought I could deal with her. Most days I had no nerve for it, no stomach at all. And I was having my own crisis, this thing about Tillie and me. Which had been going on a while, I'm not sure how long. I had gotten this idea. It was unsettling. It was all about what she thought I was hearing in the sessions. The thing about her special cries of pain, the soft murmur, the secret music, all that. The thing is, was she aware, did she have any idea about it? What if she thought I was hearing these things, something she couldn't hear? Something beyond her. Maybe I didn't hear it at all, but what if she thought I did? Wouldn't that make her listen for it? She could be a better listener than I was. She was capable. This was something I didn't expect. I started feeling there could be a combined situation, our situation, mine and hers. Listeners together, listening for the same thing beneath her words, or between her words. Of course, there was the possibility I just imagined it. Whatever was happening I was weathering it with her. At that point, it looked like it was just Tillie and me, Romano, beside the mouth of the cave, Tillie's cave. And I guess inside my own heart. Both places.

♦

One week she said, "Have I told you about William?" This was the law student she went out with for a few months. "We were serious for a couple of seconds maybe," she said. "I was ambivalent towards him." She wanted to understand it. There was an incident. She said, "Claire called me and said they were going out and did I want to come. So I guessed I'd call William, but just as a friend, and see if he wanted to go. I hadn't gone out with him for weeks, probably more than a month. It's not like we talked every day or anything. So I called him as a friend. And we're there at the bar and I'm next to Artie and he and I start talking. We weren't talking that long but after a while William stood up and said, 'Well, I'm leaving.' And I said, 'Okay, we'll talk. Give me a call.' Something like that. So he left, and ten minutes later, he's back. And he's standing behind me. And I could sort of see, you know, the steam coming out of his ears. But I kept trying to ignore him and keep talking to Artie. But William is really steaming, you know. It was so uncomfortable.

Finally Artie and I got up and left. We were going to the diner on the corner. But William follows us, yelling at me, 'You can't do this,' and stuff like that. And I said over my shoulder, 'Don't go crazy, William,' or something like that. So Artie and I go into the diner. There was really nothing between us. I realized Artie wasn't really interested and I wasn't either. But I was having a good talk with him. Let me ask you, do you think I did anything wrong?"

"It looks like William thought so."

"Yes. And I mean, he was so pushy, just standing there behind my chair and then yelling at me that way."

"What did it feel like?"

"I got kind of annoyed."

"Annoyed?"

"Well, I was trying to have my conversation with Artie and just because I went there with William that didn't mean I had to leave when he wanted me to."

"And after that?"

"I stayed annoyed. I mean, I wanted to be friends but that wasn't going to be possible. I definitely didn't want to see him after that. But you know what happened? He sent me flowers. He thought that would make everything okay, after the way he acted. There was a note with the flowers, 'Please forgive me for being such a schmuck.' I wanted to call the florist and tell them to take the flowers back. But Dinky said to me, 'Well, he's only trying to apologize. Go a little easy on him. What's the point of sending them back? They'll only just sit there. William won't even find out.' Dinky didn't realize. William was pulling me down. I didn't need that. Maybe he was going down. I couldn't help that. I didn't want to go down. I couldn't have him clinging and clutching at me."

♦

Then there was a whole story about a man she met. Now we're probably some five months into the treatment, if you could call it that. "A lot of us were hanging out at the Royale on University Place," she said. "I used to talk all the time to Seth, one of the bartenders. I thought Seth was hip, very villagey. He had his whole rap about, you know, the media and the manipulation of everybody by the forces that run everything. I'd just listen. Nothing happened between us. Thank God. Things were bad enough without that. I used to go there mostly on Friday nights. I met a guy there, Eric, who was interesting. I found him appealing. He dressed well, not like a college student. He seemed educated. Eric liked to talk about books. He liked anthropological sorts of things. But he was down-to-earth. He loved India. I think he said he'd even been there. He understood all the mythology and the gods. I liked talking with him. He usually came Wednesday nights. He said he'd lend me some books if I wanted. I said great. That made me feel good. I started looking for him on Wednesdays just as someone to talk to. So it went like that. A few weeks like that. I felt comfortable with him. And maybe we were getting closer. Anyway, I liked seeing him and I had a good feeling about him. Eric and I could talk through the whole evening, and I didn't have any classes Thursday morning, so I could stay late on a Wednesday. So one night, and again it was a Wednesday, getting a little late, and we'd had a few, and he leaned toward me and kissed me, just like that. Wow. So I kissed him back. Nothing conspicuous since we were sitting at the bar. No one was paying any attention. We laughed and did it again. Then Eric said, 'How about we get out of here, okay?' I said, sure, let me just go to the ladies' room. So I did and put my coat on and went back out to the bar. I saw Eric standing near the door. We were good to go. Then I saw Seth behind the bar cocking his head toward the other end of the bar, motioning me to go back there. I followed him back and Seth whispered to me, 'He's married.' 'No,'  I said. 'Yep. He's married,' Seth says. I asked him, 'How do you know?' He said, 'I just happen to know he is. Just ask him, why don't you?' I wanted to slap Seth across the face, but I felt more like crying. Anyway, he pointed to the back room and I went back there. He said, 'I'll handle it.' I waited there until he got rid of Eric. He came back and said he told Eric he'd best go elsewhere to pick up girls."

◆

The next week Tillie begins by saying, "You're not going to think much of me after this." What's unfolding now? I never tried to stop her. I should have. With all her negative stuff, I should have stopped her. But I always let it unfold and maybe we could figure it out it later. She launched into a story about her serving job. Tillie was explaining. "I got a job that summer at the bar, with the help of Seth. I was doing the tables in the back, just on weekends. And maybe a weekday night here or there. I had five tables, and Seth or Michael, the other bartender, they'd be doing the bar and the tables in front." The way she described it, after a week Seth asked her flatly if she wanted to skim off some money. And he had it figured out how the owner wouldn't know. Tillie was telling me this and kept saying, "Listen to me. There's something wrong with me." Seth told her they would write up the drinks on a bill that Tillie would bring to the tables. This was what he called a chit. The customers would pay this, and then she'd take the money back to the bar and Seth would ring up a lower amount on the cash register. He and Tillie would split the difference. The register was all the owner would check on. Seth would try to knock off the price of a drink or two wherever he could. If customers used credit cards or asked for a receipt or a real bill then he'd have to ring up a real bill. Tillie said she didn't hesitate. She said, "I'm not proud of it, you know. It was so disgusting." But she started doing what Seth said. She went along with the scheme for weeks and she really didn't know why. "What was I doing? It was stealing. And not just a little. I guess it was a game against the straights. That's what Seth and I thought. We were smart. And we weren't hurting anyone. It wasn't alcohol. I was completely sober. I didn't drink at all when I was working. I made a rule for myself." Tillie said she wanted to tell Kaela and she wanted to tell her father but she knew they'd be disgusted with her. She was disgusted with herself. "It was sick. I was so scared. The money was unreal. I didn't keep track. I bought clothes. I bought shoes. I bought CDs." Tillie said she finally told Seth she had to quit and she did. "I was scared to death. I couldn't take it. He said, 'What is your problem? You're being ridiculous.' I said, 'You're a real sleaze, you know that?'" She said she had to tell her father. "First I blamed Seth, then I said it was all just a lark to see if it would work and I planned all along to give the money back. He just looked at me. Dinky would go completely deadpan when he couldn't make any sense out of what I was telling him. Which happened all the time. He said, 'You know, Till, sometimes I wonder about you.'"

♦

One week she asked me, "Why do you have to know all this? I don't even know why I'm telling you all this. I should stop myself." And then she told me more. "I hope I'm not as scummy as this sounds. I wouldn't have done anything like this afterwards, believe me. It was scummy though. I didn't think it through." This involved another friend from school Tillie would talk about. "Jen had her East Side background and she was fun to be with. She liked to have fun. She was happy-go-lucky and she used to go to a lot of parties. Some pretty wild ones, it sounded like. So one Friday she asked me to go to one and she'd meet me there. I was kind of flattered. I wasn't with anyone at the time. So I go there. I'm invited as a friend of Jen's. It's in the east 80s. Big apartment. I really didn't know what to expect. I was feeling out of place. I didn't know anybody and nobody knew me. And then Jen called me and said something came up at the last minute and she couldn't make it but have fun. She told me she wanted to introduce me to Peter, the guy she was going with, and I should look for him. So I figured I'd stay a little while. Nothing very wild was happening. Just drinking and dancing. There were a lot of people. It was getting to be late. The only ludicrous thing that happened was this couple came in through a window. They climbed up the fire escape. All the way to the fifth floor. People laughed. The guy was called 'The Count.' Apparently he was known for stunts like that. And then another guy comes up to me and says, 'Hi, you're Jen's friend.' It was Peter. So we started talking. He turned out to be attractive. He was a little older. Jen hadn't been seeing him very long, maybe a few months. She liked him. So I got into a long conversation with Peter. He worked at a corporation. Apparently he did serious financial work. He had a sense of humor and I was enjoying myself. We danced a little. I was getting tired. Then we sat down and Peter took out a couple of joints and we shared them. After a while he suggested we go somewhere else and we went down and got into a cab. He suggested we go to his place farther uptown and I didn't say no." Tillie stopped talking. She wasn't looking me. After a minute all she said was, "Not good. Not good."

◆

Why don't you quit, Tillie? I wanted her to quit. I needed her to quit. Was this therapy, Romano? Never were you the great safety net, and my paranoid brain tells me you wanted me to fail once and for all. Was I ready for this? I should have quit while I was ahead, out at the lake. Would you have cared? But that's what I should have done. Because where was I with this one? There I was, listening to these scrapes and screw-ups, these self-involved tangles, letting myself in for all this crap, with this one patient. I'm trying to weather her situations with her, but never knowing what to say to her. The question is why. Why do this to myself? It wasn't good for me. I felt beat up, contaminated actually. It was hurting me, and it had to be hurting her, letting her delve into everything, spill everything. Same thing as happened with others we know about. How do you deal with it? There was this powerful merging or confluence going on. I couldn't think. You have to constantly check yourself. It was getting terribly easy to forget that. Before every session I'd tell myself, you have to keep that distance. You've got your own journey to worry about, not just hers. You can't be flowing into the other person or let her flow into you. That way lies madness. I started telling myself, just be yourself, be in your own little boat, so to speak. Along the way we can call to each other. Of course we can do that. We should do that. We must do that. We may not even see each other, but we can call out. That's what it means to be human. You call to someone and they call to you.

We cry out to them, we say go there, or I'm here, I'm over here. Across the distance. But you need the distance. Whatever it takes. One day I'm nauseated listening. Tillie is talking and her words are pouring out. I was sick to death at that point. I tried not to listen. I make like I'm drifting into my own reverie. I pick up the little wooden matchbox that I had on my desk and hold it up to my nose. Forget your story of the day, Tillie. She reacts, highly offended, "What are you doing?" "Nothing," I say.

◆

No one said it had to be easy. I asked you the best way to bounce back each week. You didn't see any problem. Anyway, a couple of weeks later I was more myself. And Tillie kept on plowing ahead. She held up two fingers. "Rich and Dinky were like that." There was something in her voice talking about the two of them. The two men in her life. "They played this game," she said. "It was too funny. They'd sit at the table and tap on each other's nose and whistle Yankee Doodle and the first one who couldn't hold out and laughed lost the game. Then they'd do it again. I never saw Dinky that happy as when he'd be talking to Rich. They could talk about baseball by the hour." She stopped and looked down at her hands clutched together in her lap. Finally she said, "The son he never had." Whole sessions were given over to praising Rich. And remembering him and missing him and feeling flattered knowing him. "He really was too good for me," she'd say. "I mean it. I didn't do right by him. But I was overwhelmed. It was like I was hit with a club." Definition of bittersweet, you've loved something and you've lost it, but at least you once had it. She'd run through the litany. He played jazz piano. He was a tennis champion in college. He read everything. He knew everything about art. She never got tired going through it. Plus he was kind and strong and real. She'd repeat, "He was the love of my life," in case I missed the point.

◆

She started a session, "I think I've been basically disappointed with life. I mean the whole bit. What it has to offer. I've always disappointed myself. I thought I could do a lot if only I could find out what to do. I never did. Life never seemed to work for me." She stopped and looked over at me. "Well, it wasn't only that. What we've said, I did it to myself. I had to run away from Rich. I didn't measure up. I didn't know what I'd gotten into." Then she said, "I guess he didn't either." She talked about their first apartment. "It wasn't easy to get. It was on Carmine Street. Second floor, but quiet. It was cute. The bedroom was just a nook off of the living room. We fixed it up. We were kind of set. So I thought we should get married. I needed it. I started hinting. Then I kidded about it. Then I just said it, 'Come on, Rich, let's get hitched.' Then I nagged him. And I nagged more. I had to. There was no reason why we shouldn't be married." She said Rich was always calm about it. He would tell her how at that moment he was trying build up his connections in publishing and get experience with freelance jobs. Then he could establish his business, and support her and himself, and maybe a family in the future. "He must have told me a thousand times, 'You know I have to focus on this.'" She said she didn't believe him. He'd remind her he was only twenty-nine and he didn't feel ready to be married. She said, "I was hurt. It was because he didn't love me. I'd throw tantrums and act nasty. I'd be silent. I'd give him a cold shoulder. I threw a glass into the sink and smashed it. I didn't care. I was impossible. Then I'd cry and fall apart and beg him to forgive me." She told me she once grabbed an expensive art book Rich had given her and took it down to the incinerator. "I left it on the floor where he'd find it when he took out the trash."

♦

You were checking in with me. You had another case for me. Remember? You said it would be a little like one of the families from the year before. "It's a good case. Not that tough. The mother's just nervous."

I said, "Uh, not just now."

"Are you okay?"

"Yes, Romano, I'm okay."

"Any problems with your case?"

"No. No problems."

"I can have her transferred to someone else if you want."

"No. It's good. It's good."

"I'm glad to hear it. It's been good having you back with us."

I said, "Check back with me in a couple of weeks. Or how about give it a month? You know how it is." I thought I handled myself quite well. I'm sure you saw through me. We both stood up. That's when you said, "What kind of material does she talk about anyway?"

"Well. Right now, her marriage, what happened there. She gets into it."

"That's got to be grist for the mill. What does she tend to do with it?"

"She's coming to grips." What a practiced liar I'd become.

"Right. Coming to grips. Well, we're running a clinic here. You'll keep me posted?"

"I'll keep you posted," I said.

◆

Then there was the briefcase. "I have to tell you what happened with Rich's briefcase." And she went on. "This was four years ago. It was winter. Rich had his briefcase stolen at the college. He left it by his desk and walked out of the room without it. It was gone when he went back a couple of minutes later. He was frantic. He went nuts. He looked in all the other classrooms on the floor and asked everybody he saw. Luckily his laptop was in his backpack. When he got home he collapsed in my arms." Tillie was telling me this and started tearing herself apart. She said, "Of course I felt terrible. I did. But I began putting him down. He wouldn't stop carrying on about it. I thought he was blowing it out of proportion. First I said, 'Enough already, Rich. You've done all you can.' And he had. He reported it to the college, he put up notices. I really didn't want to think less of him, but I did. I thought he was acting weak. He should have been tougher. He carried on about it for days. I was cruel. I mocked him. I said, 'Oh, don't be a damn baby, Rich. Stop whining. Give it a rest. It's not the end of the world. You think nobody ever lost their stupid briefcase before?' And why? Why did I have to be so mean to him? Over some stupid thing. He would never have done that to me. He'd look at me with a sad look. He said, 'I lost a lot of work.'"

◆

And another time, it was more about Rich. "I could get pissed off, you know. I did want to take care of him. I really did. He deserved that much. He deserved much more than that. But sometimes I wanted to be alone. We might have been different that way. And I couldn't just say to him, 'Look, I'm not like you, I need alone time.' I'd feel like I was doing something wrong, feeling that way. I always felt like I was hurting him. He seemed to want togetherness all the time. Always whenever we were at home. It was irritating. I hate to say that. But it's true. Like I enjoyed doing the housework by myself. The cleaning and the vacuuming. I didn't mind doing that. But Rich would butt in. No, that's not kind. He wanted to help. But it went a lot better if I did it by myself. I liked getting it done and at least I could say, I did this. But he'd follow me around, moving chairs, getting in the way. It distracted me. He'd say, let me vacuum the living room and I would, but he'd miss places. I didn't want to insult him, but I did. I remember saying, 'Don't you get it? How many times do I have I tell you, I'd rather do it myself? You do a lousy job.' Of course he'd look hurt. He wouldn't say anything, but I know I hurt him. Or mopping the floors. When it had to be done, he'd want us to work side by side. But, no, how about you do the bathroom, I'll do the kitchen. We don't have to be side by side. But I gave in. I did it his way most of the time. It was his neediness, I hated that. And then the stupid laundry. I once snarled at him, 'Forget it. I'll do it. You don't know what to do. You're always asking me how to do it, what do you do next, what clothes go where, etcetera. Just let me do it, all right?' That was the last time he asked me if he could do it."

♦

Tillie's train story came a little later. The crazy woman who frightened her and rattled her and bruised her feelings. "I'm on the A train going downtown. It's really packed. I was holding onto the pole in the middle near the doors and I spotted a handle to grab in front of some seats. I made my way over there. It was only three or four feet away. There was this woman holding the strap next to mine. She was tall, way overdressed for a weekday and overly made-up. So she said to me, right to my face, 'That felt good, did it?' My heart stopped. I said, 'I don't know what you're talking about.' And she said, 'Of course you don't.' I think I said, 'What?' She said something like, 'You know you pushed me.' She never stopped smiling. She kept looking at this man standing against the door. He must have been with her. She was showing off for him. By then I realized she was crazy so I just looked down. My heart was pounding. A young girl on one of the seats looked up at me. Her face told me she'd heard the lady and knew she was crazy. I just stood there holding the strap for a few stops not looking at the weird woman. I was shaking inside. Finally a seat was empty behind me, farther away, and I took it. At least I stood my ground and didn't move away from the woman right away. I told Rich when I got home. He was so tender, saying how awful I must have felt. He held me. He said over and over, 'I'm so sorry that happened.' He knew me. He was so good about it."

◆

"Mindy and I always got together for our birthdays." Tillie was telling me about the night she got drunk. She was saying, "We both had our birthdays in October. Usually we had lunch. This time we made it a dinner date and went to Giordano's. Great food and wine. And we were having a good time, like always. Rich was getting a series wrapped up. That's actually why I was out. He needed to concentrate. I didn't worry about him  But I called him. I told him all was well by me and how was he doing.

Everything was good. Then I called him again. I said I was going to be a little later than what I said before. I'd be home by eleven the latest. And that was fine, that was cool. And then it must have gotten to be ten or ten-thirty. . . ." Tillie stopped. A smile came to her face. Then she said, "Can you imagine? I look over at the bar and Rich is there. He's sitting there just looking over at us. There's Rich. He smiles at me and I make my way over there. 'Hi,' he says. I asked him what the hell was going on. He said, in his wonderful voice, 'You know, maybe it's about time to go.' I said, 'How long have you been here?' He said, 'A couple of minutes.' So we paid the bill and got into a cab. We dropped Mindy off. I was very drunk. I got quiet. I couldn't say very much. We got home and I threw up. He sat on the bathroom floor with me and stroked my back."

◆

 She needed to piece it together. I wasn't helping her. Like where did this fit? The night she was spaced out at a dinner. She said, "I didn't remember half of it. I don't know what happened to me." She said it was hard to describe. "My head was in a weird place." She went on, "I was with Rich and it was important to him. Not that he wanted to impress anybody, but he was close with all of them. He worked with them. He respected Jean. It was her dinner, she was about to start another job. Also, the Goodelles. They all loved Jean. The Goodelles were giving her this dinner, to wish her good luck." Tillie frowned. She looked up at me with a lost look, like I might have the answer to something. I had no idea what could be coming. Then she said, "First we sat around talking in the living room. There was wine, which I didn't have any of. Rich was glad about that, I imagine. I might have sipped a little water. I was starting to feel, I mean I was starting to realize that I was feeling funny. They were talking about work. I felt left out. I visited the bathroom and thought I looked normal. So maybe I was. Except my vision. It was a little blurry. And my head was heavy. It was unpleasant. So we sat down at the table and everyone was laughing and in a good mood. Now I feel okay and I thought I'd be fine. I was beside Rich. Sarah Goodelle is next to me on my other side. She's serving around the food. It's some kind of soup to begin with. And it's put in front of me. I didn't touch it. Which was okay. Sarah laughed about the ingredients or something. And then the real food came, which was excellent I guess. But I realized I couldn't eat."

I asked Tillie if she was sick.

"No, not like that. It's that I couldn't eat food that night. I couldn't face it. I don't know why. I was blocked. I couldn't eat. I told Rich. He said to try just a little, or something like that. I said, okay. But I knew I wasn't going to be able to. I took a spoon of the soup and put it to my lips. He watched me. I couldn't take any into my mouth. I couldn't even take a taste of it. I was afraid I'd throw up."

I asked her what was going on.

"I don't know. For some reason I didn't want to eat. My stomach was turning over and over. I just couldn't face taking in any food. I guess I was too nervous."

"So what did you do?"

"I whispered to Rich and I think we both told Sarah. Rich wasn't happy about it. The wife who couldn't eat. The others saw me. They saw me not eating. I don't know. I just could not eat that night."

◆

"Rich always tried to fix me," she said one day. Like she was broken. She'd told me that before. Rich said the city was hurting her. He thought the pressure was getting to her. "Like when I told him how I slipped on the ice in front of the building and I'm sitting flat on my ass on the sidewalk while people walk around me, both women and men. That kind of thing. He worried about me. He said these things were taking a toll on me. Or that woman on the train. It was all the wear and tear. Or when they did work in the apartment above us and a ton of dust came down into the living room. Not to mention the noise." She said Rich wanted them to get away, get out of the city and go to a safe, quiet place. "He started this thing about us moving," she said. "He talked about the place upstate where he grew up. It was peaceful. It was safe. We could get a house. He said I'd like it. Rich just really wanted us to be happy. That's all. That's the truth." He told her he could do his writing anywhere and she thought that was wonderful. "But I had to tell him I hated the idea of moving. I told him, 'I can't be uprooted like that. We're here, I'm here, you're here, Dinky's here. To do something like that? I don't know what it would take. I never heard of that place of yours.' I told him over and over, not in a nice way either. It really started to piss me off. I wasn't fair. I was a bitch."

♦

She was talking about the time Rich wanted to go on a writing retreat. "It was for a weekend in New Hampshire," she said. "I wanted him to go. It was summer, it would be great weather. But I worried." She started calling him once he got there and got settled in the house. "I called too many times. Morning and night. I got lonely. I could tell I was bothering him. It made him worry about me, him being all the way up there. He was mad at me. He thought I was acting dependent. He was right. He was the strong one and I was the weak one. I know that." Tillie was looking at me. I should have told her she was strong, too. And she was. But the way I was feeling, it would have sounded hollow. After a minute she went on. "Rich had another retreat coming up that fall. I begged him to go. I begged him and I promised I wouldn't call. I told him, 'Go, Rich. Please go. Have a good time.' But he wouldn't go. He was worried about me. So you see? I was hurting him." Then she said, "Dinky tried to help me. He praised me every time he saw me. He said how great it was I'd met Rich. He was so glad we were together. But one night I had to let it out and be honest with him. We were standing in the kitchen. It was after eleven. I told him I didn't think it was going to work out." She described it. "God, I never saw Dinky like that. He didn't raise his voice or anything but he was really upset. He had his mouth tight. He said, 'What are you talking about? You just can't think that way.' I said, 'What would you have me do?' He asked me if he should talk to Rich. I said, 'That won't do any good. I'm sorry, I'm trying to tell you, your daughter is . . . I don't know what I am. A lousy, rotten wife.' Then he sat down and so did I. He looked very tired. He said, 'But you love him, Till.' I didn't know what to say. Finally I said, 'There's just too much of my shit getting in the way.' He had to hear it. Then I said, 'I do love him, I love him to pieces.' Dinky looked so sad. He really loved Rich."

Hearing it, you would have felt just like I did.

♦

Her face was drained and she was talking to the wall over my head.

"I guess it doesn't matter."

"What's that?"

"What?"

"What doesn't matter? You said it doesn't matter."

"It doesn't."

"What doesn't matter, Tillie?"

"None of the things we talk about."

"Why? Why are you saying it doesn't matter?"

"Because it doesn't."

"What are you thinking?"

"Nothing, really." She glanced at me and looked away. "I don't know."

She still wasn't looking at me. I had a sense she wanted to look up at me, but her head was bent down and she studied her knees. She let out a long breath. Then she said, "I'm sad about Rich." I didn't know what to say. She sat there. She was holding her feelings in. After a few minutes she said, "I can't talk about it."

◆

You came by my office, I guess making the rounds. "Cyril? I wondered how you were doing."

"I'm all right," I said.

"Things going okay with Tillie?"

"I think so. She's suffering, Romano."

"What's happening?"

I wanted to tell you about the cries. Do you remember? I said, "Well, the cries are there. Very strong. I think they've been there from the beginning. Her cries of pain and confusion."

"You're feeling that again?"

"Yes. All her feelings of loss. I'm hearing all of it. She feels so alone. She talks and I'm hearing it."

"Yes, I know your thinking on that."

"I actually feel honored and privileged, you know. I'm trying to make it work, pull it together for her. As hard as it is. For both of us."

"Look, if it works for you, it works for you. We all have our approaches. You know mine. I suppose this is yours."

"It's not easy. It's never predictable. The cries aren't always there. You try to sensitize yourself and stay open."

"I guess."

Then I asked you, remember? "Why wouldn't it work for you? If you got into it." I was longing for comradeship, I guess you'd call it. Something we could share, you and me. I thought we'd be able to share this.

"Unlikely."

"I think it just might work for you. If you can really listen to someone, it will work."

"Now you're going to say you want me to try it."

I said, "Why not? Try a different way. You could do it."

You said, "Well, it's unlikely. I won't say it's impossible. I've tried weirder stuff."

I said, "Maybe you'll think about it?"

"I don't know, Cyril." What were you thinking? I couldn't read your expression.

I said, "Anyhow, Tillie and I go along. It's difficult with her."

"Well, it's what we do. That's it. They come in, we try to help and we learn."

I never knew if you were humoring me or what was happening. Whatever it was, I felt you gave me something.

◆

Tillie would tell me about her fears. She called one of them her fogginess. She said this one was quite scary. "I still get it sometimes. I don't know what it is, but I can get completely foggy about where I am. And I can never tell when it's going to come over me. It's like I get lost in a thick fog. I don't really see where I'm going. No, that's not it. Because I see everything okay. Have you ever been in a building that you've been in before but you've gotten onto the wrong floor? So you know where you are but it's not the way it should be from the floor you actually know? It's like that."

"This happened in buildings?" I asked.

"It might have. But it's mainly outside. It'll just take over. It was probably a year ago I happened to be in the village going uptown for something. It was still morning. So I get on the train. And I know the station, West 4th Street, from when we lived on Carmine. The train is rattling along just fine. I'm feeling tired, but not too bad, maybe just a little foggy. But I know where I'm going. The train makes a stop and I look up and see where we are and we're all the way out in Rockaway. It happened just like that. I didn't know where I was. It was unbelievable. I was scared. It's like a nightmare and you're swept away to a strange place. I'm always a little afraid getting on the subway. I have to force myself. Plus there are days I can't even bring myself to leave the apartment."

◆

Another fear she had. "I don't think I ever did this," Tillie said. "I just felt on the verge. It was nervewracking. I went through this terror about five or six years ago."

I said, "Terror sounds pretty bad."

"I guess you'd call it a terror. Come to think of it, it pretty much stopped after Rich and I got married. It all passed, I got rid of it. But memories come back, they come and go. Sometimes I won't think about it for months, but then it might get on my mind. I didn't tell Rich and I didn't tell Dinky. It just seemed so, I don't know, indecent. I haven't talked to anybody about it. But I wanted to tell you. You're going to think I should be in the loony bin."

"Try me," I said.

"It was like this. I'd be standing near somebody, okay? This is back then. It could be anywhere, on the street, in a store. I think it was mainly women but men too, and I'd imagine running toward them and banging into them, just bumping into them a little."

"Bumping into them?"

"Yes, I really thought of doing that. Isn't that weird? I'd see myself running into a person and just bumping them. I remember it would come into my head. And then my doubts. Because back then, during the problem, I could never be sure if I'd done anything or not. Can you imagine that? I had such shame about it. And I felt like people knew. They could see my impulse. Like I didn't have any skin, like my muscles and nerves were all exposed. You know that freaky woman on the train? I didn't do anything. I didn't. But five years ago, I couldn't be sure. I'd think maybe I did do something. I had this for about a year, I think."

"That's a long time. What happened?"

"It got less and less. But the thing is, back then, it wasn't just bumping someone and losing control like that. It was not being sure. It was being afraid I might have already bumped someone. This was almost worse, feeling I'd already done it. You know what you're doing now, and you can stop yourself, but how can you be sure about the past, what you did in the past? You can't. Maybe you already did it. That's the bitch of it. You're not sure what you might have done. Is that insane, or what? What did I do, what did I do, kind of thing. Worries about what I did on my part. I remember thinking about it. If I'd done that, there must be specific examples when it happened, you know, and I'd be able to remember them, if I sat down with a pencil and paper. I thought I should do that. But you realize, you just don't know. How many people was it? If you did it at all. You don't know. If I did something like that it would be like temporary insanity, right?"

"Maybe so. It's hard to say."

"I mean, that's not appropriate behavior by any standard. The worst of it was, you know, I worried about whether I'd done it with people I knew, certain people, even friends. That would be terrible, the worst. A lot of nights I was up worrying. What if I'd done that to someone I knew?"

♦

The next week she was a half hour late and she looked a wreck. I asked if she was okay. She said, "I don't know. I don't feel good. I mean, it's rough. I don't feel right. I don't feel whole. I don't feel good about myself at all."

I said, "Tell me a little. What does it feel like?" My only thought was she should keep talking.

She said, "It's something wrong. I don't know if it's guilt or what it is. I'm not a bad person, but you know what it feels like? Like I'm never doing the right thing. Every morning I wake up feeling that way. It colors my day. I feel uneasy. I feel like I deserve to be punished. I don't know for what. It's for something I did, or didn't do. It's not strong. It's not overwhelming. It's just always there, just way back there in the back of my mind. And it makes me sad. Sad, sad. I don't know what I've done or who I've hurt. Is it someone or everyone? Or I'm disappointing them. Not living up to what I should be. That's more what it is. I've let people down. So many of them. Like Dinky and like Rich. They expected better of me. And also people I don't really know. Incidents come to me at night. All the memories. Things I should have done, or things I did wrong. And you know who I've let down the most? Me. I have my moments but they don't last very long. And I wonder, will I never feel any better? I hate to even ask, because I know the answer. There's a shaky area inside. It's not right. What's the use of fooling myself? I'm tired of it. I really am. Tired, worn out. I feel like everything has fallen through. I gave up asking what makes life even worth it, worth the trouble, worth anything. Different things for different people. I never knew what it should be for me. I never knew the real worth, did I? You know that, you've seen it for a long time. I never reached that high point. People must say, that's it, that's what I want out of life. I guess it feels great for them. But then look at what they're satisfied with. I know, I know, it's the inner feeling, not the trappings. Doesn't mean anything anyway. Nobody's life is like mine. And what is mine like? Not much. Except I'm sad. If I sound bitter, you must be right. I am bitter."

◆

In the very next session she said, "If it weren't for Dinky and Rich, I might just do it. I would do it. Punch my sad ticket. I should've done it already."

That got my attention. I said, "Are you serious?"

"You think I'm joking? I'm not joking. I feel like I need relief. It's too much."

"So you are serious."

"I don't know if I am."

"What do you mean?"

"There's Dinky and Rich. They'd never get over it."

"Of course, they wouldn't. They love you, Tillie. They need you around."

She said, "They'd blame themselves."

"They'd blame themselves, and they'd never understand how you could do such a thing."

She said, "They would never understand. You understand, though. Don't you?"

I thought about what to say. I said, "I'm afraid I do."

"Thank you, Cyril." I said nothing. Then she said, "It passes through my mind. You must have heard that before."

"Like what passes through your mind?"

"You know. You think how it's a good, easy escape. No more suffering. You'd never know a thing after that. It's all over. You'd be dead."

"So you've thought about it quite a bit."

"Leading up to it, that would be the worst part. You'd be thinking all these things. How it would affect certain people. People you love. And others. You couldn't get away from that. But it happens all the time. I've heard about people who check into a hotel with a bottle of wine and the pills, or whatever."

"Do you ever have a plan like that?"

"I imagine it. I run through the scene."

"But don't do it, okay?"

"Are you worried about me?"

"Yes, when you talk this way. Of course, I'm worried. I'm scared. I'm afraid I'm not doing enough for you."

"Does it look that way? I guess it does."

"I get afraid something's missing for you here."

"I guess I haven't been talking about the right things."

"No. That's not true at all. Don't say that."

"I don't think I've been talking about the right things. I can see it in your face."

"Tillie, you've been talking about all the right things. We just need to keep going. We're on the right track."

"I don't think so."

"Yes. We are. Believe me."

She asked, "Do you mean it?"

I said, "Yes. I do."

She said, "I guess I'll believe you."

♦

A week or two after that Tillie asked, "So what do you think?" She was holding her head, leaning forward, with her elbows on her knees, her two hands cradling her cheeks. "I'm sure you never heard so much . . ." Her voice faded. She closed her eyes. After a minute she came to life and said, "I need to tell you about my saintliness. That was something."

"Saintliness?"

"Yes, saintliness. It was something bad I went through. Very bad."

"What was it?"

"I thought maybe I told you. Did it start when Rich was away? Or was he just very busy with a project? I don't know. I know we weren't cooking after a while or anything, just ordering in. I wasn't eating much. Then I just drank milk for a week. I'm sure that's how it started. It was a mind thing."

"What do you mean a mind thing?"

"It was all these doubts I was having. I started worrying about my existence. Everything really. I saw that the world was right in front of me, but I couldn't touch it. Everything had gotten unreal. It was interesting. It wasn't so much who I was, but was I really there? I felt wispy and weak."

"Could you say more?"

"I've always been what you'd call self-conscious. Like what are people thinking of me. How do I seem to them. Kind of thing. Like I wonder what you think of me."

"You've asked me that," I said.

"I know. This was more of the same. I started watching myself. I was watching Tillie from outside of Tillie. It was like I was someone else watching me. I still do that, but not like then. I worried how I seemed. So it went on, and what do you do? You just feel very self-conscious and you judge yourself. It's very inhibiting."

"I guess we all do that," I said.

Tillie went on. "It was when I talked, too. I started listening to myself. It was like listening to an echo. Something like that. I'd be saying something but it was like hearing another person. Some things I was saying weren't what I'd normally say at all. They weren't me. It got worse and worse. I didn't want to talk. It wasn't me talking. You see what I mean?"

I said, "Yes."

"Who was deciding what came out of my mouth? It wasn't me. Was it written by someone else? I don't know. I had no control. Except not to talk. It was bad. I couldn't say my own thoughts."

I said, "That does sound strange."

She said, "So, yeah. And where was I? If it's not me talking, where was I? I lost myself. I wasn't as real as I should be. I couldn't use myself. I knew what reality was. I did. Absolutely I did. The only thing is, I wasn't part of it. No, wrong. I was part of it. Reality is what's there. I was always there. I don't know. I never disappeared or anything like that."

"So what happened?"

She said, "I thought I figured something out. Now this is going to sound more crazy. Bear with me. I can explain this. It came to me one night, in the middle of the night. The idea flashed into my head.  What makes things real is being good. If something is real it has something good about it. And vice versa. I was up for hours with it."

I said, "So you're saying being good makes things real?"

"Yes, and the better things are the more real they are. Something like that. Like I might think this is a good room for talking which would make it real. You see what I mean?"

I said, "I think so."

"So that's what I realized. That was the way to be real. Just be good. This made sense. I got control. I knew what I had to do. I had to be a good Tillie, the very best Tillie. But it wasn't easy."

I said, "I don't imagine it was."

She said, "It wasn't. It wasn't easy at all. I had to be good, but good like a holy person. I had to try to be a saint."

I said, "Ah. So that was the saintliness."

"Yes," she said. "That was the saintliness, that was the saintliness." Her voice had gotten farther away. Then she said, "But not just try to be a saint."

"No?" I said.

"No. Not just try." I waited. A half a minute went by. Then, very quietly, she said, "Not just try. It was already true." Her voice broke. "I was a saint already."

She bawled like a baby, Romano. She was bent over and her head was on her knees. She broke down and wept like I've never seen anybody weep. It was heart-breaking. Her back was heaving with sobs. I don't know how long it lasted. I knew I couldn't do anything. Finally she managed to calm herself.

She said, "I was in a daze. I cut off all my hair. I was a holy woman. That was my day. I called it Great Saint Tillie's Day. That was the day Tillie was a saint. I put on a nightgown and started to parade out to the nearest church. Rich stopped me. Poor, poor Rich. Great Saint Tillie's Day. Dinky came and got me."

It was harsh, it was depressing, it was disappointing. The turn you took. It shocked me after some of the things we'd been talking about. But I should have expected it.

"Cyril, you need to give up all that. Your cries and everything. It can't be good for your patient and it can't be good for you."

"What? Why are you saying this?"

"I think you should move on. I'd like you to move on. I think you should."

I said, "What are you talking about?"

"You're stuck in this. You've got this one angle you use. You know it's not accepted. You need to develop yourself in other ways. Don't you think?"

"No, I don't think. What are you getting at? I thought you understood what I've been doing."

"I understand it. You've told me. It probably gives you the feeling you're helping this one patient. It's all about your feelings for Tillie."

"I know it's helping her."

"I'm sure you feel that. But you have to admit it's limited in terms of helping most people."

"I disagree."

"Are you making progress? I assume you are."

"Yes, we're making progress."

"It's deepening?"

"It is."

"Tillie's just one case, Cyril. There are others I want you to see who aren't appropriate for your approach. Maybe some short-term cases? Your approach wouldn't be appropriate."

I said, "It's more flexible than you might think. But I don't think you understand what I'm trying to do. You just don't."

"Well, if you're flexible. That would be good."

I said, "Right now I'm just trying to help Tillie."

You said, "Okay, Tillie's a good patient. But, you know, the clinic has others coming in. And, by the way, you know the model I base my work on is pretty widely accepted. There's a lot of data behind it."

I said, "Right. But you know what? This model, that model. I think something else is bothering you."

"How do you mean?"

"Why don't you like what you're hearing, Romano?"

"What I'm hearing is fine. It's fine. But it's not going to work across the board."

"We don't know that. But you're so negative. What's going on?"

"What do you mean?"

"It sounds like it would be a threat opening yourself like I do, or try to do."

"No, I think I'd know if I felt any threat."

I said, "Would you? I'm not going to sit here and be your analyst, but it could be hard to tolerate."

"No. That doesn't sound right."

"Really?"

"Really."

"Okay," I said. "Let it go. I didn't mean to step over a line."

You said, "No problem."

♦

The cries, Romano. The cries. I couldn't deny them, whatever you said. Cries from the depths of the cave. The sad secrets that were striking me dumbfounded or something. And they did. They must have. I wasn't imagining them. They were too real. I felt I was hearing them again. For me to feel that again, they must have been there. It was like a sound you just barely make out in the background, a low voice underneath the chaos. Yes, it could have been just like that. They were there in that soft voice of the real Tillie crying out her special griefs and joys and sorrows. All her pain, all her mistakes, the regrets, the longing, the confusion. And the things she put a lot of others through. Her family, the heartache of the marriage. Which was so vague to me, you know. Her love was so powerful but so painful and uneasy. She was crying out for closeness and warmth but somehow missing it. And I was hearing all this. You knew how it went with her sessions. Always hard to sit through. Impossibly hard. You never look forward to one of them and it's always a relief when it's over. But don't forget, whatever you thought, weren't these the things we all cherished from the early days? All of our people, all of them, would have envied me and respected the mystery. They should have been told about it. But no, that would not have been good. Just like for you and one of your patients, this was between Tillie and me. It had to be.

♦

Tillie was circling around and back to the loneliness. Some days it was all she could talk about. She said, "I knew I was alone. That I knew for sure and certain."

I said, "Didn't Rich call?"

"Yes, but we didn't see each other."

"You wanted to?"

"Of course. But it wasn't the right time. It was a bad time. At least I talked to him. I missed him so much you wouldn't believe. But the burden I'd gotten to be." She stopped and looked at me. Then she was looking through me. She said, "It's inside me, this loneliness. I carry it everywhere. I feel it everywhere. I remember sitting with Rich. I'd be sitting right next to him, our arms around each other, and I'd be feeling so lonely. Isn't it funny that it could come out that way with Rich? He loved me so much, and I loved him. I still do. But I don't understand. Just when we were closest it comes out. That's the saddest thing. I mean, Rich was there, but I needed someone who wasn't there. Someone else. I'm always asking myself, who could it be? Probably my mother. I'm always longing for her. Just when I'm not thinking it'll come over me. I should have gotten used to it. How much did I know her? Not enough. That makes me so sad. But how much does a little child know its mother? It's not the knowing. It's the warmth, the love. It's being wrapped up in the love, that's how you know her. That's what you miss. But, you know, this loneliness, I kind of study it. You wouldn't know what it's like. The dreary feeling. It's a desolated feeling. I don't know how many people have this. Couldn't be very many. I feel completely alone. I mean completely. It's like I'm alone on a train at night, you know, going somewhere endlessly. I don't even know where. By myself. No one else is there. No one. That's how desolate I feel. It's a rainy night. No one else is on the train and it won't ever stop or ever get to anywhere. Somehow I've gotten on a train like this and I don't know why I have to be here. All I can do is look out and stare through the rain at the night."

◆

It was only a week later when she started in on herself. "I'm so ashamed. The things you know about me. The ugliness. The filth. Everything. All my filth, all my ugly trash. Not one good thing." And she started to weep, very quietly, in her moaning way. "I've disgraced myself, Cyril. I can't stand this. And you, how could you let me do it? Spill my guts this way. I've said too much. Is it all in my file or something? What did you write about me? Can I see it?"

"Tillie, Tillie. Slow down. It's all right."

"No, it's totally disgusting. I never did one good thing. Not one single thing. Hurting people. I should have cared. I didn't. I'm hard. And I treat myself like the filth that I am."

"Tillie. What's going on with you? For God's sake."

"You know it. You heard all of it. That's what I did. Acting like a whore and a thief and a liar. A worthless addict. Abusing people. I was destructive. I didn't control myself. Being female and using it. Risking people's lives, even the wreck up in the country. Pushing people around, manipulating. Pushing my friends until they get disgusted. Never mind what's right for them. But I never listened to people. I've hurt people and didn't even know it. Not even see them as people."

"Tillie. Please. What is this? You're feeling so much pain. You need to take a step back. Take some deep breaths."

"No. I'm selfish. That's me. I failed Rich. I wouldn't let him be himself. And he counted on me. He needed me. He had nothing but love for me. But I let him down. I'd never compromise. I had to have things my way. I didn't trust him or anyone. Why couldn't I trust? If I became a hundred saints, I'd never be able to make anything good out of it."

"Tillie. Just stop now. Will you? Just stop."

"What did I learn in all the time I'm here? Tell me, what did I learn? I'm a child, I'm a bad child.  Leaning on people, using them, turning my back, deceiving, getting high. Everything just for me. I wanted from people and when I didn't get what I wanted, I used them. I was a user all right. Just false. Playing tricks on people. The trick was on me."

"Tillie." I reached out for her hand.

She yawned violently. "Sorry. I've been up most of the night." She just looked at me. She was huddled there, helpless, her hands clutched between her knees.

I said, "You're caring, Tillie. That's who you are. You know that. You're concerned about people."

"No. The people I ever helped are few and far between. I knew I was a user. But knowing what you're doing is no excuse. You never saw me. You don't get it. Now you know. Now you know me."

"I do know you, Tillie. And you're not these things you're saying."

"You don't need all this from me. I'm a burden around your neck. I'm sorry I ever started. Putting us both through all this."

"Look, Tillie, you're in pain right now. Just slow down, will you? It'll get better. It's okay, believe me."

"It's not okay."

"It is okay, Tillie. It is. You're okay. I know you. Believe me. You're a good person. Don't you think I know you after all this time? You're doing everything right. You're open. You try to get to the truth about things. In good faith."

"How do you know? I've lied a lot. I have. That's just the way I am. I'm sorry we ever met."

"Oh, Tillie, don't say that! Don't say that! I'm not sorry."

"I have to leave you, Cyril."

With this, just this, I was lacerated. I couldn't hear it. I didn't want this. I didn't want it to happen like this. I was shouting at her. "What are you saying?"

"I've got to stop seeing you."

"No, Tillie. No! You can't do that. What's happening? Will you tell me? I don't understand." I got up and went to her. I leaned down and took both her hands and pulled her up. I was looking into her face. She looked tormented. Her eyes were filled with tears. I was clutching her hands too hard and I let go and stood there. She fell back and was silent.

"Look, Tillie. You're not quitting. I won't let you. We aren't done."

"We are. We're done."

"Don't say that!" I sat down on the couch next to her.

"Cyril, I'm a hopeless case." She lay her hand on my arm. I put my hand on hers. She squeezed my arm. Then she took her hand away.

"You're not a hopeless case."

"I am. I'm hopeless. And you know why? Every time I have a chance for love I can't help myself. You've seen me. I . . . screw it up." She bent her head down to her chest and wept.

"But Rich hasn't gone away."

"Oh, yes he has. He's gone."

"You're not sure."

"I'm very sure."

"Listen to me. Listen to me! You're going to feel better. I know it. We can make this work. We're getting there. We'll figure it out, we'll do it together." She was silent. "Talk to me, Tillie."

She didn't raise her head. I put my hand on her shoulder. "Tillie, you've got to talk to me. We can't give up. Not now. Make a nothing out of the whole thing? No. I can't let you do that. I care about you. I won't let you do that. Look at everything you've put into it."

"I have to go away, Cyril. I have to. My father's taking me away. I'm sorry. You did your part. I didn't do mine."

"Tillie, NO! Please, Tillie! We have to stay with it. We're not failing. Jesus! Can't you see that? Can't you see it?"

But she couldn't see it. She couldn't. We were both weeping when she left.

♦

Then I gave up. You knew about it. I gave up for a time. I was shattered. So much lost. I'd been emptying myself for so long, giving what little I had to this helpless, frightened, lonely person. And wasn't she the worse for it? With all her confusion and shame. And trust me, I'm haunted by it. Now and always. Haunted by the chances I missed. To do anything for her, anything at all, never mind anything healing. Never an idea what to do. But do something. Torturing myself with every useless vision of what I might have done. And missing her. You can't know. You never knew her. Later trying in desperation to find her and her family but failing and failing and failing and finally refusing to let it go but having nothing left inside me for the effort. And sure, feeling the anger, the disgust, the revulsion, the maddening irritation, hating the things she did, things to drive you wild, different things I could hate in myself. For a while I thought she was in charge of herself. Troubled, yes, but she seemed whole. She was moving ahead. Until I listened more and heard more. The cries were there. I told you. She had her beautiful, beautiful strengths, but the cries were always there, inside all the things she talked about, all her strivings. And then, along with everything, my doubts and my nightmares came. These came even before that last time. Nightmares and terrible thoughts and memories. And the horrifying thoughts about you, Romano. If you were somehow involved in the ruin. Could you have said something that frightened her? Like she'd been with me a long time. Could she have heard that as a warning? She wasn't doing well and I wasn't doing well and she was hurting me? I don't know why that came to me, but you might have said something. I know you wouldn't do it to hurt me. Threats from you? That makes no sense. And besides. Even if you had said something and Tillie distorted it, misconstrued it, you couldn't help that. I've played through that last time. I've combed through it, the way she turned on herself, combing through it, and thinking it was like her but the violence was too intense. She came out so exaggerated with it. And with so much rage. Wasn't that too much even for her? But no. That was Tillie. In a terrible crisis, but it was Tillie. She could do that. I don't doubt she was feeling all of it. The wild exaggerations? I have no idea why. She could distort things. We know that. She was in a terrible place. Terrible beyond her control. But, still, she would never try to destroy our precious treatment, all our work. Not if she'd been herself. All the trials and the tears we shared, those were ours. At the end I believe she entrusted them to me. They were mine for safekeeping. She knew I'd always be their guardian. But the wrecked treatment, that had to be my own doing. And I know you meant well. I know that and I've felt it. I felt it in my heart from the beginning. Because of who you were and who you had always been. You were good, if only I had dared to know you. And, after all, who were you? That's something I wanted to tell you. You were the angel, Romano. You should know that. You were ever and always the angel who saw me. You saw me in all my anguish. And you listened. Not willingly, I'm sure, but you were there. But so terrifying for me when I knew nothing. Could I risk even approaching the aura and the power? Could I risk even knowing all you gave me? I know you gave me patients who were good for me, who made me grow one way or another. I came to understand that. You gave me Tillie and I was grateful. The wretched travail didn't matter. Or it did! That was what mattered the most. Because it gave me my feelings. So you heard my cries. You must have heard them as I felt the pain and the wonder, bringing me up against myself, causing me to suffer and to learn. All of it made me live. And live with that impossible intensity that we have no words for. We have no words for it except love and pain, those worn out tokens. Oh, and that other one, loss. And we needn't ask about her, if she felt any of it. The cries from her heart were under it all. They were there that last time. And I'd been hearing them for a long time. But I didn't do enough or I did the wrong things. I didn't help her piece it together. What was she all about? Why couldn't I find out? Explore, ask, probe a little more, help her get some distance. Help her through. But I pulled back. I was afraid to plunge into that whole confused, chaotic world. I knew fragments, or I thought I did. That was all. Week by week it seemed to slip away from me. So, it was me. I'm the one who failed. First we have to keep them in treatment and then help them see why they want to leave. Why they want to leave. Believe me, I've pondered that one endlessly. And I hated her blaming herself. It looked like she was her own worst enemy. She wasn't, and even so, who hasn't fallen in the mud along the way? And fallen again and again? She could never forgive herself. She never saw herself, the lovely girl, the lovely young woman who cared so much for people and who had the most rare passion for life. And she was telling me so many of her hopes. For herself and for Rich and her father. Hopes that they could all be together. Hopes she could make her family happy. I've seen her weep that she couldn't do more for them, that she didn't know more about their work. And about them, too. She was so sure she had failed them. But she vowed again and again to do better and have a good life with them. She wanted me to know this. She was trying to fight free of her misery and have a life. Even in the midst of her distress, even with everything weighing on her, she wanted to live. And it was a life she wanted me to know. She opened it to me in all its beauty and all its torment. Week after week she offered it to me. The grand things she spread out before me, the gardens and the fields and the bright sunny prospects. But she didn't even know and maybe she'll never know all the beauty I found in her and in the dance and harsh music of her struggle.

*The End*

New Yorker since college, Joseph Adams has been a college teacher and a psychotherapist. *The Cries* is his first novel.